MW00785379

Amazing
Interview
Answers

---

44 Tough Job Interview Questions
with 88 Winning Answers

by
Richard Blazevich

ISBN 978-0-578-54732-9

www.amazingjobskills.com

Amazing Job Skills Publishing
Dallas, Texas

Introduction

The fact that you're reading this book suggests that the stakes are high. Perhaps you're anticipating an interview for your dream job or trying to get into a competitive school. In any case, you may recognize that impressing an interviewer is the next crucial step in your career.

You'll be relieved to know that interviewing is an easy skill to master. You don't need physical strength or superior intellect. You just need a game plan and time to practice. In this book, I'll give you a game plan. With it, and with some practice, you can quickly learn to give amazing interview answers and get offers for the jobs you want.

While interviewing hundreds of candidates over the years, I've seen interviews that fall into three categories. About 70% are disappointing. Unprepared candidates struggle through their interviews with answers that are either vague or don't address the questions I ask.

About 20% of interviews are good. Candidates are prepared, and they respond to most questions with clear, relevant answers.

Finally, about 10% of interviews are amazing. These candidates answer every question with poise and confidence. Their responses are riveting, and I wish I could interview them for hours. This third group will breeze through life getting whatever jobs they want.

In this book, my goal is to help you be amazing in your future job interviews so you can be in that top 10%.

Most amazing candidates are not naturally gifted. They don't have super powers that enable them to answer any question that they are asked. Their secret is preparation. They know which questions are typically asked during job interviews, and they're prepared to answer those questions.

During business school, I became an amazing interviewee, as did many of my classmates. We knew exactly which questions to practice because recruiters told us the questions before they came to campus. We would spend a few hours every week practicing our answers to those questions, either on our own or in study groups.

We practiced because our professors and other students told us the importance of preparing for interviews. Unfortunately, most students don't get that advice. Many schools teach everything but interview skills. When students graduate, they may be prepared to do their jobs, but they are not prepared to get their jobs. The good news is that this book will teach you the interview skills that you should have been taught in school.

I'll explain how the approach I used in school will help you become an amazing interviewee. I've included 44 interview questions and sample answers for each question. You'll get a total of 88 sample answers to get you started. Your interview answers should be customized to your experience, but these sample answers will point you in the right direction.

What a rush it will be when you conclude interviews knowing that you nailed them. If you follow the steps in this book, you should experience that feeling every time you complete an interview.

You can also use these skills to be more persuasive in every aspect of your life. Not only do interview skills help you get the jobs you want, they help you persuade people to see your point of view in various situations. I haven't changed jobs in years, but I use my interview skills every day. I use them to get more resources at work; I use them to explain new concepts to my daughter; and I use them to give advice to friends.

While this book focuses specifically on the interview process, I encourage you to also check out my other book, *Interview Prep Playbook*. It includes tips for every step of the job hunting process including developing your job search strategy, preparing your resume, and practicing your interview answers.

One more thing: This book is intended to be a workbook. I've included space for you to write information about the jobs you want. There's also room in the back for you to write your personalized answers to common interview questions.

Some people think it's inappropriate to write in books; not this book. It is a tool for practicing your interview answers. Therefore, please highlight text, take notes in the margins, and use the templates in the back of the book to compose your amazing answers to the sample questions provided.

I hope you enjoy this experience. Now, let's get started.

Contents

Getting Started

Preparing for the Interview

Many candidates think of an interviewer as an opponent. They think the interviewer is hoping they will fail. Nothing could be further from the truth. An interviewer is more like a reluctant judge in a contest. They're hoping to find someone who meets the criteria of the contest. Once they find a worthy candidate, they're happy to select that person and award them the prize of a job offer. That way, they can end the interview process. An interviewer wants you to succeed. They want you to win the contest so they can hire you and get back to their regular job.

Your goal should be to make it easy for the interviewer to select you as the contest winner. You want them to envision you in the role they are trying to fill. To do that, you should tailor your answers to the role. If the role requires creativity, you should highlight your creative skills. If the role requires organization, tell them how organized you are.

In this book, I'll show you a range of answers to the most common interview questions so you can see how to tailor your responses for specific jobs. You should never use the specific answers I give you in this book. Hiring managers can tell when your answers aren't sincere. Instead, use the sample answers to inspire you. Then, craft your own answers based on your personal interests and experiences.

To become an amazing job candidate, you should do three things: research the type of role you want; research the specific job you'll interview for; and practice your answers for the six most common types of questions. The first two topics are covered in this section. The third topic is addressed in the remainder of this book.

Step 1: Research the Type of Job

Research is surprisingly simple. You can find thousands of sample job descriptions on the internet. If you know the type of work you want, just find a sample job description and write down key responsibilities related to that type of job.

This will help you prepare answers that will set you apart from other candidates. Once you know what employers are looking for, you'll know how to best answer questions during your interviews.

Here are examples of job details I found during a quick search on the website for the U.S. Bureau of Labor Statistics:

For **sales representatives,** responsibilities include working with potential and existing customers, meeting sales objectives, and building lasting relationships.

For **graphic designers,** responsibilities include working with design software, creating compelling visual concepts, and preparing graphic files for production.

For **bookkeepers,** responsibilities include working with accounting software, documenting financial transactions, and developing financial recommendations.

Now, take a minute to research job descriptions for the type of position you want, and summarize the details below.

Job Title: _____

Responsibilities: _____

_____

_____

_____

Step 2: Research Job-Specific Details

If possible, get a job description for the specific job you want. Often, employers will post job descriptions online where they post job openings. If you can't find a job description online, contact someone in the company to request it. Often, hiring managers or human resource representatives will be happy to send you a job description prior to your interview.

Read the job description and make notes about the responsibilities. This is your cheat sheet for formulating your interview answers. Getting the job description is like getting the answers to a test before you actually take the test. Employers usually tell you exactly what they're looking for in the job descriptions. You need to frame your answers to highlight your skills and experience that will make you successful for performing those responsibilities. Here is an example of job description highlights:

For a **paralegal** position, specific responsibilities might include researching laws and regulations, writing reports to help attorneys prepare for trials, and filing briefs with the court.

Throughout this book, I'll show you how to use your job description summaries to frame answers to interview questions. Remember, your answers should be customized to the specific job you want, so use the employer's job description to practice the answers to the upcoming test.

Now, you can use this format to update the job details for the specific position that you want:

Job Title: _____

Responsibilities: _____

_____

Step 3: Prepare for 6 Types of Questions

Most interview questions fall into one of six categories. While there are variations, preparing for these six types of questions will help you succeed in almost any interview:

1. **Experience Questions** ask about your background, education, and work experience. A common example is, "Can you tell me about yourself?"

2. **Interest Questions** ask about your interests. One example is, "Why are you interested in this job?"

3. **Fit Questions** help interviewers determine if you'll be a good fit for their open positions. "What is your leadership style?" is an example of a Fit question. These questions are sometimes called *Behavior* questions because they often ask how you might behave in specific situations.

4. **Case Questions** test your knowledge and thinking skills. For example, if you're applying for a consulting job, the interviewer might ask, "If your client is losing business to a competitor, how would you approach that challenge?"

5. **Odd-Ball Questions** test your ability to think on your feet. An example is, "If you were an animal, what type of animal would you be?"

6. **Closing Questions** capture information interviewers might need before making a final decision about you. One example could be, "Is there anything else I should know about you?"

I've organized this book based on these six types of questions. In each section, I'll explain what employers are looking for, the questions they typically ask, the frameworks you can use to answer questions, and examples to inspire you for your responses.

In the back of this book, I've included additional sample answers and worksheets for you to complete. If you use these templates, you should be ready to give amazing answers to most interview questions.

Dos and Don'ts

Here are a few tips for all types of interview answers:

Do:
- **Be positive**. You should focus on the positive aspects of your experiences. Employers want to hire people who can be positive in any circumstance, so show them that you can do that.
- **Be passionate**. Employers want to hire people who really want to work. Show them that you enjoy the type of work that they are hiring for.
- **Be specific**: Employers want to hear specifically what you've done and the results you've personally delivered.
- **Be concise**. Your answers should be long enough to get the interviewer interested in you, but not so long that they think you're monopolizing the conversation. Most answers should be less than one minute, and you should never give an answer that takes more than two minutes.
- **Be grateful**. The interviewer is taking time out of their day to talk with you. Let them know that you appreciate their time and their consideration. You should start the interview by thanking them; end the interview by thanking them; and send a thank you card or email after the interview.
- **Give examples**. There's a great saying: "Facts tell, but stories sell." People remember stories, so tell the interviewer

stories about what you've done and what you've accomplished. The stories should be brief, but include enough detail so the interviewer can envision you in that situation.

- **Use frameworks**. In this book, I'll show you several useful frameworks that will help you structure your answers to any type of question. Using a framework will prevent you from rambling or being vague during interviews.
- **Be honest**. You should be truthful in every response. Not only is it the right thing to do, but interviewers often do their own fact-checking on their top candidates. If you say that you accomplished something, and they find out you didn't, you could end your chances of ever working for that company.

Don't:
- **Don't be modest**. Interviews are not the place to be humble. You should proudly talk about your biggest accomplishments, your most relevant work experiences, and any major awards you have won. Interviewers like to hear about results and accomplishments, and they love meeting confident candidates.
- **Don't be personal**. Don't talk about personal information such as family, friends, and hobbies that are unrelated to the job. Don't talk about religion, politics, your favorite sports teams, or any topics that could be polarizing.
- **Don't be negative**. No matter how bad your previous jobs or bosses have been, don't say anything negative about them during an interview.
- **Don't be verbose**. Don't go into too much detail in any specific area. As you practice your interview skills, find a

brief way to answer each question so you're providing an amazing answer without repeating yourself or droning on with unnecessary details.

Experience Questions

Experience Questions Overview

Interviewers typically start by asking about your work experience. These questions help them assess whether you have the basic skills needed to do the job. If you're prepared for these questions, they're the easiest to answer. If you're not prepared, they can be the most difficult.

Experience questions give you the chance to set the tone for the interview. They also give you a chance to distinguish yourself from other candidates.

Here are the most common experience questions:

- Tell me about yourself.
- Walk me through your resume.
- Why should I hire you?
- Why are you a good candidate for this job?

I recommend you use a P-E-N framework for these questions. P-E-N stands for Passion, Experience, and Next. This approach will show the interviewer that you're a better choice than typical candidates who provide vague or irrelevant answers to these questions.

Often, a hiring manager will interview a dozen or more candidates for an open position. Many candidates will not leave a lasting impression. With the P-E-N approach, you can start an interview by making a strong first impression so the interviewer will see you as a top choice from the beginning.

P is for PASSION:

Start by telling the interviewer what you are passionate about, and make sure you choose something that is related to the job. They want to hire someone who enjoys their work, so let them know what you enjoy. Here are a few examples for different types of jobs:

A **bookkeeper** might say, "I'm an organizer. I really enjoy organizing things into neat, orderly groups."

A **sales person** could start by saying, "I've always loved building relationships with other people."

A good starting point for a **graphic artist** could be, "I love being creative."

Now, go back to the job-specific details that you identified during Step 2 in the previous chapter. Then, figure out what passions you have that relate to the responsibilities on that list.

E is for EXPERIENCE:

Summarize your experiences that are relevant to the job. You should do this briefly without going into too much detail. This will give the interviewer context for the rest of the interview. Here are examples for various types of jobs:

For a **marketing manager** position, you might say, "I have a bachelor's degree in marketing from Northern State College. After graduation, I worked at Sizzle Advertising Agency where I developed digital media campaigns."

A **cashier** could say, "I've worked in two different retail jobs over the past eight years. At Fashion Forward Clothing Store, I started as the assistant cashier and was promoted to head cashier. Then, I worked as head cashier at JC's Supplies."

Someone applying for a **police officer** position might answer with, "I have an associate's degree in criminal justice. While earning that degree, I worked as a security guard for a large office complex."

Look over your resume, and think about your work experiences that are most relevant for the job you want. Then, practice summarizing those experiences into a few sentences.

<u>N is for NEXT</u>:

Tell the interviewer the type of experience you'd like to get next. Your answer should be directly related to the role they're trying to fill as described in the job description. Here are examples for your N:

An **office manager** might say, "I'm looking for a role that will allow me to leverage my organizational skills and provide opportunities to supervise others."

A **financial advisor** could conclude with, "Next, I'd like a role where I can grow my knowledge in the area of retirement and estate planning."

A **school teacher** might respond, "I'd like to find a position that allows me to build lesson plans and teach students math skills since math is my favorite subject to teach."

Now, here are examples of using the P-E-N framework to answer common interview questions.

1. Tell Me about Yourself

"Tell me about yourself" is a question you are likely to hear during an interview. An interviewer is seeking high-level understanding of your interests, experiences, and communication skills. Your answer will set the tone for the rest of the interview. If you nail it, the interviewer will see you as a compelling candidate, and they'll be rooting for you for the rest of the interview.

If you bomb this question, it will be very difficult to recover. The interviewer may mentally rule you out, and they'll look to reinforce their conclusion as you respond to other questions.

The good news is that this question is the easiest to prepare for. Since you've already researched the job description, you know exactly what the interviewer wants to hear. Your answer should highlight your interests that directly relate to the job.

Don't fall into the trap of telling the interviewer about your personal interests. They really don't care what your favorite hobbies are. They want to know why they should hire you. Once they hire you, they might start caring about your interests, but until then, focus on your attributes that make you a good choice for the job.

You should briefly summarize your relevant work experiences, and you should tell the interviewer what type of position you want. Naturally, your desired role should be exactly the same as the role that you're interviewing for.

Here's an example of an amazing response to this question for a **marketing assistant** position. Responsibilities for this job might include identifying marketing campaign ideas, writing agency briefs, and managing cross-functional project teams.

PASSION: "I've always loved finding creative solutions to challenging problems."

EXPERIENCE: "When I was in college, I worked on our yearbook staff, where I led a project to create the first-ever online version of our school yearbook. I also had a summer internship where I created the social media sites for three non-profit organizations.

"When I graduated from Southern State University with a bachelor's degree in marketing, I went to Way-Cool Creative Agency where I developed marketing campaigns for clients, wrote project briefs for our agency teams, and managed cross-functional groups that included people from insights, graphic

16

design, project planning, and client relations. I've been working for the Way-Cool Agency for three years, and during that time, I've been promoted from Assistant Account Manager to Associate Account Manager. I also won the agency's award for the most creative marketing campaign."

NEXT: "Now, I'm looking for a role where I'll have more responsibility for making marketing decisions, and where I'll be able to find creative solutions to increasingly challenging problems. I really want a role that involves identifying marketing campaign ideas and managing cross-functional project teams."

I really like this answer because it touches on all the candidate's experiences that are related to the job they're trying to get. If I'm the interviewer, this candidate is making it very easy to see that they have the skills and background to be successful in this role.

2. Walk Me through Your Resume

"Walk me through your resume" is almost identical to "Tell me about yourself." You can use the P-E-N framework for both questions.

For this question, I like to see candidates summarize each section of their resume by providing highlights from the Education and Experience sections. Typically, it's best to provide a chronological summary of your most relevant experiences.

Avoid the temptation to read your resume. The interviewer doesn't want you to recite things that they can read themselves. They want you to tell them the highlights in your own words.

Here's a sample answer to this question for a medical **sales representative.** Responsibilities might include building relationships with healthcare providers and selling a portfolio of medical supplies.

PASSION: "I've always had a passion for building relationships."

EXPERIENCE: "As you can see from my resume, I have a bachelor's degree in chemistry from Western University. While I was there, my peers elected me to be the president of the debate club. Hopefully, this shows that I can both build strong peer relationships and be persuasive.

"After graduation, I worked at Wheaton Labs, where I started as a Laboratory Assistant in their medical supplies department. I quickly learned that my passion was in selling ideas, not working in a lab. Their director of sales recognized my passion and gave me a chance in the sales department. There, my performance was in the top 10% of my peer group, and I've been promoted from Assistant Sales Representative to Associate Sales Representative."

NEXT: "Now, I'm looking for a role where I can have more responsibility for a broader line of products. I want a place where I can build lasting relationships with customers and help them succeed using products that I believe in."

I love the way this candidate shows they have the background knowledge for this role. They also do a great job of explaining why they made a career switch that took them closer to the job they now want.

3. Why Should I Hire You?

"Why should I hire you?" is another common question. Please don't answer this with, "I will work hard" or "I'll do a good job." Your goal is to differentiate yourself with a specific, relevant answer. Give a clear example that shows why you're a better fit for the specific role than other people who are applying.

Here's an example of an amazing answer for an **insights manager.** Responsibilities for this job might include analyzing marketplace trends and competitive landscapes, identifying business opportunities, and recommending improvements to marketing programs.

PASSION: "I've always loved finding new ways to grow a business."

EXPERIENCE: "I understand that you're looking for someone who will research the marketplace and study consumers to identify business opportunities. I've demonstrated those skills when I was an Insights Analyst at Highbrow Salons. We were losing share because consumers were choosing smaller, niche salons. I researched the issue and identified a segmentation strategy that led to a new marketing approach. I then designed and executed the research plan that identified our new marketing message and social media strategy. That led to the company's first year of sales growth in over five years, and they've grown every year since they implemented the new campaign."

NEXT: "If you hire me, I'll bring that passion for growing a business and my skills for researching the marketplace to your team."

In this answer, the candidate does a great job of connecting their passion to the role that they want. If I'm the hiring manager for this job, I'm looking for candidates who can demonstrate their ability to identify ways to grow my business, and this candidate has done exactly that.

4. Why Are You a Good Candidate?

An interviewer may ask "Why are you a good candidate for this role?" so they can see if you understand the role. They want you to show a connection between your skills and the job that they're trying to fill.

This question is very similar to "Why should I hire you?" so you can use the P-E-N framework to answer it. Here's an example for a **sales manager** job at a car dealership. Responsibilities for this job could include managing team of sales representatives and motivating team members to deliver results.

PASSION: "I understand that you want to build a high-performance sales team. I have a passion for that, so let me tell you why I'm a great candidate."

EXPERIENCE: "In my current job, I manage four sales representatives. When I was promoted into my role, the team was struggling to reach their sales goals. I met with each team member, determined the best role for them on the team, and restructured our responsibilities so each person could play to their strengths. I found that one team member didn't have the skills we needed, so I had him reassigned to another role in the company, and I hired someone else with the exact skills we needed. Over the two years I've been in my role, my team has gone from having below-average results to being the highest ranked team in our department."

NEXT: "I'm looking for a role where I can have a bigger

team and more opportunities to grow a company's sales. You should hire me because I've demonstrated my ability to build a high-performance sales team, and I can do that for you here."

I love the way this candidate brings teamwork into their answer. They show their ability to assess talent and get the right people on the team. They also show compassion for someone who wasn't a good fit, and a willingness to get that person into a role that was better for them.

5. Why Did You Leave Your Last Job?

Employers might be curious about your reason for leaving jobs. They want to hire someone who will be around for a while, so be prepared to answer why you left each job that you've had.

Typically, we have a number of reasons for leaving a job, so focus on the reason that demonstrates that you'll be a better fit for your new job than you were for one of the jobs you left.

Good reasons for leaving jobs include wanting more responsibility, shifting your career direction to focus on something you have passion for, or moving to a new city for family reasons. These answers indicate that you have ambition, passion, or family ties to the location where you're job hunting.

Bad reasons include not liking the people you worked with, being bored with your job, or leaving because you just felt like making a change. With these answers, employers might see you as someone who is difficult to work with, easily dissatisfied, or cursed with a short attention span.

Here's a winning answer for a candidate who has changed jobs several times and is applying for a **medical assistant** position. Responsibilities for this job might include interviewing patients, recording medical histories, and assisting with patient exams.

"I have had three different jobs since graduating from high school. When I was getting my associates degree, I worked part-time as a personal care assistant for an elderly woman. I enjoyed that job, but it was not possible for it to become a full-time job when I graduated, so I left for a full-time position.

"My next job was as an orderly at a hospital. I loved working with the patients and medical staff, but I wanted more responsibility, so I accepted a job as a medical assistant.

"After working at that job for two years, my husband got transferred here to Cleveland. Therefore, I'm looking for medical assistant jobs here. I really love working as a medical assistant, and I'm excited to find a place in the area where I can make a contribution to the organization."

This is a strong answer because each job change has brought the candidate closer to the job they are interviewing for. The employer can see that the candidate has a passion for the work, and they're doing well with their current employer. However, the role they want is a better fit for their career plans or personal needs. Therefore, they are likely to stay in the new job longer than they stayed in previous jobs.

6. Your Favorite Job

I love asking candidates about their favorite jobs. It's a great way to see what they enjoy and assess whether they're a good fit for the open role.

When answering this question, pick a job that has similarities to the one you're interviewing for. Also, be prepared to answer why you left that job.

Here's a good answer to the question for someone applying for a position as an **arbitrator**. Responsibilities for this job might include facilitating communication between disputing parties, clarifying issues and interests of involved parties, and guiding discussions to mutually acceptable agreements.

"When I was in high school, I was a student counselor. I loved that job because it was so challenging. Students would come to me with all kinds of issues, most of which related to conflicts with friends, family members, or faculty.

"I found that I really enjoyed helping people work through conflicts. It was very rewarding to help my fellow students see things from other people's point of view. Then, they could resolve issues in ways that benefited both sides.

"That led me to pursue an associate's degree in counseling. And now, I'm looking for a place where I can start my career and pursue my passion for helping people resolve conflicts."

I really like this answer because it shows that the candidate has a passion for something that is specifically related to the open role. It also shows that the candidate has taken the steps necessary to prepare for the desired role.

If you get this question during an interview, think about the jobs you've had that have prepared you for the job you want. Then, highlight the attributes that demonstrate your passion and skills for doing the job well. Again, if it's not obvious, explain why you left the job. In the example above, an explanation is not needed since it's implied that the candidate left upon graduating from high school. If your reason for leaving isn't obvious, go back to Question 5 for suggestions on how to address this topic.

7. Your Least Favorite Job

The question, "What has been your least favorite job?" can be very tricky. The interviewer may be trying to see what de-motivates you. They want to ensure that you won't be turned off by an important element of the available job.

I recommend you choose a job that is as unrelated to your desired job as possible. Most of us have had jobs that were a terrible fit for us. Pick one of those, and explain why the role you want is a better fit.

Here's a strong answer to this question for a **waiter or waitress**. Responsibilities for this job could include greeting customers, answering questions about menu items, preparing itemized checks, and taking payments from customers.

"One summer, I worked as a bookkeeper at a small tourist resort. I'm good with numbers, so I thought it would be a good job for me. However, it was not a good fit at all. I love being around people, and I enjoy moving around while I work. At the bookkeeping job, I sat at a desk all day and there was no interaction with other people.

"While I worked there, I had extra time so I worked a few shifts as a waitress at the resort's restaurant. I loved that job, because I enjoy serving people. It also gave me a chance to move around while I worked, which I like doing.

"Now, I'd like to find a role where I can be around people, serve them, and move around while I work. Hopefully, being good with numbers will help too since I'll be taking payments from guests."

One thing I love about this answer is how the candidate focused on a positive outcome. It's tempting to dwell on negative aspects of your least favorite job. Avoid that since interviewers avoid hiring negative people. Take this question and show how you can turn an unappealing job into something positive.

Experience Questions: Dos and Don'ts

When an interviewer asks you to tell them about yourself, you may think they want to hear about your personal life. They don't. They want to hear why you would be a good fit for the job. Limit your answers to information that directly relates to the job unless they indicate they want to hear about something else.

Do:
- Use the P-E-N framework (Passion-Experience-Next).
- Limit your answers to two minutes or less. Your answers should be long enough to get the interviewer interested in you, but not so long that you're monopolizing the conversation.
- Make sure your Passion is directly related to the job you want.
- Briefly summarize your work experience. This should be done in four to eight sentences. You'll have time to go into more detail later in the interview.
- Be positive. You should highlight the positive things you've learned and accomplished.
- Mention your biggest accomplishments, your most relevant work experiences, and major awards.
- Mention promotions. Interviewers like to hear that you've earned increasing levels of responsibility.

Don't:

- Don't include personal information, such as details about your family, friends, or hobbies that are unrelated to the job.
- Don't mention your religion, political views, or favorite sports team unless that information is specifically relevant for the job. Unless you're applying to work at a church, on a political campaign, or for a sports organization, these topics are far too polarizing to mention during an interview.
- Don't be negative about anything. No matter how bad your previous jobs or bosses have been, don't ever say anything bad about them during an interview.
- Don't go into too much detail in any specific area. The interviewer wants to see that you can summarize information without getting caught up in details. Show you can do that by providing high-level answers here; then go into the details later in the interview.
- Don't spend time talking about experiences that are irrelevant to the job you want. Employers want to know why you're a good fit for their open role. They don't want to hear about your unrelated work history.

For reference, here is an example of how not to answer an Experience question like, "Tell me about yourself." This candidate is applying for a **marketing assistant** position with responsibilities that include identifying marketing campaign ideas, writing agency briefs, and managing cross-functional project teams.

"I'm from Montana, and I'm a very outdoorsy person. I grew up hunting and fishing, and I still like to do that when I can. I went to college at Montana State University, and I ran track while I was there.

"I then moved to Denver, where I became a huge Denver

Broncos fan. I still like to watch their games, and I look forward to seeing them get to the Super Bowl this year.

"I have a wife and two children. My oldest is a bit of a bookworm, and she's doing very well in school. My youngest is more of an athlete, and she has a passion for soccer."

While this answer helps the interviewer get to know the candidate as a person, it does nothing to help the candidate get the job. The answer included no relevant work experience; it didn't reference career accomplishments, and it didn't explain why the candidate is interviewing for the job.

Now, take a few minutes to go to the section of this book titled **Workbook Section** starting on page 121, and start filling in the templates provided there. Remember to frame your answers in ways that highlight your relevant accomplishments for the specific job you want.

Interest Questions

Interest Questions Overview

An interviewer may ask a few questions to gauge your level of interest in the type of work they have to offer. They want to find someone who will be with the company for years, so they may ask questions like the following:

- What would you do first if we hire you?
- How soon could you make an impact here?
- Why are you interested in this job?
- What are your goals?
- What would you want from this job?

For some of these questions, the P-E-N framework is very effective. For others, I recommend a framework called the 30-60-90 Day Plan. It outlines what you might do in your first 30, 60, and 90 days at the company.

I love seeing candidates use a 30-60-90 Day Plan. In one recent interview, a candidate walked me through her 30-60-90 Day Plan, and I was blown away. While some of her ideas weren't practical for our specific situation, the fact that she thought through her approach gave me confidence in her level of interest. Here's how it works:

30 DAYS:

Explain how you might quickly meet your team members, learn about the business, and define your priorities.

60 DAYS:

Show how you might start delivering results and influencing the agenda related to your projects.

90 DAYS:
Show how you might start leading initiatives with strategic importance to your department and developing new ideas for improving the overall business.

8. What Would You Do First?

If an interviewer asks you, "What would you do first if we hire you?" don't say, "PARTY!!!" They're not asking for your preferred way to celebrate. They're trying to determine whether you'll have an immediate impact or if you'll need a lot of training to come up to speed. You want to show them that you're ready to hit the ground running so they don't have to hold your hand as you learn the business.

Here's an amazing answer to this question for someone applying to be an **office manager** at a doctor's office. Responsibilities might include organizing office operations, assigning clerical tasks, and training staff members.

"I'm glad you asked. I took the liberty of creating a 30-60-90 Day Plan to show you how I might approach this job."

30 DAYS: "In the first 30 days, I'd like to meet everyone in the office and hear their suggestions for how I should approach my role. I'd also like to learn your processes for booking appointments, billing, and maintaining medical records."

60 DAYS: "In the next 30 days, I'd like to identify and implement a few ways to ensure that we have a strong team culture. I'd also like to come up with ways to improve our processes."

90 DAYS: "In the 30 days after that, I'd like to ensure that all staff members are getting the training they need to be more effective at their jobs. I'd also like to make changes in roles and responsibilities for staff members based on their capabilities and interests.

"Here's a print-out of the 30-60-90 Day Plan that I prepared for this interview. Do you recommend I change anything?"

By ending your answer with a question, you can get the interviewer into problem-solving mode. You're acknowledging that your plan may have opportunities for improvement, and you're inviting the interviewer to help you with it. If they engage with improving your plan, they'll be invested in seeing you succeed.

9. How Soon Could You Make an Impact?

An interviewer might ask this question to see if you're prepared to hit the ground running. They may need immediate results, and they want you to tell them that you're prepared to deliver.

This question is also a good fit for the 30-60-90 Day Plan framework. Here's an amazing response to this question for someone applying to be an **events planner.** Responsibilities for this job might include developing agendas, negotiating contracts, and managing event timelines.

"I plan to have an impact immediately. Since I've been an event planner in this area for seven years, I know the local venues and agencies well. I took the liberty of preparing a 30-60-90 Day Plan to show you how I might approach the role if you hire me."

30 DAYS: "In my first 30 days, I'd like to meet with everyone in the company who is involved with big events. I'd like them to tell me how event planning has been done in the past and we can discuss ways to improve it. I'd also like to start planning an event immediately so I can learn your approach through a real-world experience."

60 DAYS: "In the next 30 days, I'd like to manage progressively more complex events. I'd also like to implement improvements to make processes easier and to make your events more impactful."

90 DAYS: "In the 30 days after that, I'd like to evaluate the capabilities and contracts for the agencies that are typically involved with our events. I'd like to see if they have any capabilities that we're not leveraging or any opportunities to save money in the contracts.

"Here's a print-out of the 30-60-90 Day Plan that I prepared for this interview. Do you recommend I change anything?"

I like the way this candidate shows eagerness to learn in their first 30 days. Then, they show a clear plan for progressively taking on more responsibility the longer they are in their job. This shows that they understand the learning curve involved with joining an organization, and they show a desire to learn quickly.

10. Why Are You Interested in this Job?

An interviewer may ask, "Why are you interested in this job?" to gauge your level of commitment. They want to hire someone who will stay in the role for years so they don't have to go through the interview process again.

The P-E-N framework works well for this question, as you can see from this answer for an **agency account manager** position. Responsibilities for this job might include managing relationships with clients and planning projects related to the development and execution of marketing programs

PASSION: "I've always had a passion for building creative solutions to challenging problems."

EXPERIENCE: "When I was getting my bachelor's degree in business management from Eastern University, I worked in a marketing agency as a summer intern, and I loved it. They hired me after I graduated, and over the past three years, I've been promoted from an assistant account coordinator to an account manager."

NEXT: "I want to work for your company because I'm looking to continue my career progression in an agency that encourages cutting-edge thinking and creativity. For example, I love the campaign you did for Premier Sporting Goods, especially the way you integrated the short-form videos for their martial arts gear with the online store that you've built for them.

"Also, I have a friend who works here. She's told me about your team-oriented culture and rapid-iteration approach; that culture and approach perfectly fit my collaborative, action-oriented style. She's also explained that you have some of the best creative minds in the industry, so it's a great place for people who want to find creative solutions to challenging problems. This is exactly the type of environment that I want."

This is an amazing answer because the candidate shows a passion for something that is very important in this job, which is building creative solutions. If you're asked why you're interested in a job, be sure to explain how your passions and experiences align with the role you want.

11. What Are Your Goals?

This question can be tricky. You need to show that you want the job and that you'd like to advance once you get it. However, you want the interviewer to see that you have realistic expectations. I've seen candidates blow this question in both directions. Some candidates have shown little interest in advancement, which makes me think that they'll be complacent in the job. Others show too much ambition, which makes me think they'll be demanding promotions constantly. Your objective should be to express the right combination of eagerness to advance and willingness to put in the time to earn those advancements.

Here's an amazing answer that shows motivation with realistic expectations for an **architect.** Responsibilities for this job might involve creating building designs, preparing project reports, and researching building code requirements

PASSION: "My goal is to become a highly-skilled commercial architect."

EXPERIENCE: "As you can see from my resume, my education and certifications have given me a good foundation."

NEXT: "Now, my immediate goal is to join an architecture firm where I can continue to build on that foundation. I'd like to gain experience in CAD applications, project budgets, and building code requirements. I'd like to be in a firm where I can apply that experience and expand my responsibilities over time. I want to grow into a Senior Architect or Project Manager, and eventually, I hope to become a Partner. I know that will take many years, but I'm committed to making it happen."

This is a great answer because it shows a willingness to work hard, an understanding of the job, and a desire to grow over time. This candidate clearly did their research on the career path for an architect. The answer shows balance between a willingness to do the work needed in the current role and a desire to progress at a realistic pace.

Avoid answers that could make you seem either unmotivated or overly ambitious. If you tell the interviewer that you don't have specific goals, they will think you might be lazy or unfocused. If you tell them that you want to be running the company in a few years, they won't take you seriously.

12. What Would You Want from this Job?

If you've done your research, one of the easiest questions in any interview should be, "What would you want from this job?" The interviewer is checking to see if you want the type of job that is available. Your answer should be straight out of the job description.

Here's a sample amazing answer using the P-E-N framework of a **tax accountant** job. Responsibilities for this position might include preparing tax returns, meeting with clients to discuss tax matters, and conducting training programs for tax regulations.

PASSION: "I've always loved training people."

EXPERIENCE: "In my current role, I'm the resident expert on the software programs that our firm uses to prepare tax returns. I enjoy leading training sessions for that software, and I'd like to do more of that."

NEXT: "In my next job, I'd like to apply my knowledge of federal and state tax returns and computer software to train people to be successful in their jobs. I'd like to build the capabilities of everyone in the department so we can be a high-performance team. I hope that includes leading regular training programs that cover both tax regulations and software programs."

While this answer seems obvious given the job description, an interviewer would love to hear an answer like this. It's surprising how often candidates answer questions with responses that are vague, unrealistic, or unrelated to the role that they're interviewing for. For example, for entry-level jobs, I've heard answers such as "I'd like a job where I can set my own hours" and "I want to be promoted quickly."

With this question, the amazing answer is as simple as paraphrasing the job description. Also, make sure you tell the interviewer that you want to learn and build your skills. That way, they know that you're motivated to do the job well.

13. Make Yourself More Effective

An interviewer may ask you, "What do you do to be more effective at your job?" They want to see if you're motivated to improve your skills. Interviewers love to see candidates who seek knowledge and find ways to be better at their work.

Here's an example of an amazing answer for someone who wants to be a **creative director** for a chain of flower shops. Responsibilities for this position might include training staff on floral arrangement designs, meeting with clients to determine floral needs, and designing new flower displays.

PASSION: "I love finding new ways to express my creativity and share my ideas with others."

EXPERIENCE: "I search YouTube, Vimeo, and DailyMotion every day to find ideas for new flower arrangements. I also follow a number of bloggers, and I've started producing my own videos about arranging flowers. You can see my videos by going to YouTube and searching for the Whimsical Flower Girl."

NEXT: "In my next job, I hope to have a team that I can train on new flower arrangement techniques so we can always be coming up with ideas that will surprise and delight customers."

This type of response will let an interviewer know that you love the type of work so much that you'll always be looking for ways to do a better job.

14. How Did You Hear about Us?

"How did you hear about us?" This seems like a simple question that should have a brief answer. However, it's a great opportunity for you to distinguish yourself from other candidates. If other candidates say, "I found you through an online jobs site" and leave it at that, you can impress the interviewer with an answer that shows your commitment to the company.

Here's an answer for this question using the P-E-N framework for someone applying to be a **teacher**. Responsibilities for this position might include creating lesson plans, teaching students, and maintaining order in the classroom.

PASSION: "I've always wanted to teach at a school that has a strong sense of community."

EXPERIENCE: "I've been a substitute teacher in the Centerville School District for three years. I've been looking for a school where I can become a full-time teacher since I earned my Education degree from Western State University. I haven't had the pleasure of being a substitute teacher at your school yet, but several of my colleagues have. They've told me how impressed they've been with the staff here.

"I've read newspaper articles about your progressive approach to lesson planning, and I like what I've read. I've also read through your website and Facebook feed, and I love the sense of community you've built.

"I found out about this job because I regularly review your job postings hoping to find a role exactly like this one."

NEXT: "Through my extensive research, I'm convinced that this is a place where I can be a great fit and become a valued member of your teaching staff."

As you can see, this candidate did a fair amount of research before going to the interview. This answer is far more impressive than responding with, "I saw your job posting on Monster.com."

Before you go to the interview, review the company's website, read their social media posts, find recent news articles about them, and try to speak with people who work at the company. That will set you apart from people who just see an employment posting and apply for the job.

Interviewers love to see that you put effort into your job search, especially when that effort is targeted at their company. It appears that you're likely to stay with them if you do the research needed to determine their organization is a good fit for you. Therefore, answer this question with details about your job search.

Interest Questions: Dos and Don'ts

Employers love to interview candidates who are passionate about the work they have to offer. It is important to ensure that your answers reflect your passion. You can do this by showing that you've researched the job and you believe that it's a good fit for you.

Do:
- Tell your interviewer that you're interested in the role. Tell them what you want in a job and why their job will provide those experiences.
- Be clear about your career goals. If you don't know what your career goals are, figure them out before you start interviewing.
- Think about the jobs you've had in the past. Make note of the things you liked most about each job. Then, tell the interviewer how their open position will help you build on the experiences you've had in the past.
- Prepare a 30-60-90 Day Plan before the interview. Bring a written copy of it so you are prepared if there's an opportunity to share it. This will demonstrate that you're proactive and excited about the job.
- Be realistic about your goals. Interviewers typically prefer candidates who want to advance in their careers. However, too much ambition can be a bad thing. Show the interviewer that you want to progress at a pace that is reasonable for the role.
- Talk about things you do outside of work to advance your skills. Interviewers love to see candidates who are so passionate that they spend spare time building their skills.

Don't:

- Don't push your 30-60-90-Day Plan on the interviewer. You don't want to seem pushy, and you don't want to take over the interview. Let the employer control the topics and pace of the interview. If you pull out your 30-60-90 Day Plan too early or when it's not warranted, the interviewer may perceive you as overly aggressive.

- Don't be negative about anything. Even if the interviewer asks you about your least favorite job or your worst boss, find a way to talk about what you did like. If you dwell on negative things, the interviewer may think that you'll be impossible to please.

For reference, the following is an example of how not to answer an Interest question like, "What would you do first if we hired you?" This example is for an **office manager** at a doctor's office whose responsibilities include organizing office operations, assigning clerical tasks, and training staff members.

"Well, I'm guessing that your billing system is probably a mess, so I'd have to fix that. I have a friend who is a bookkeeper, so I'd get her involved in creating a better billing system right away.

"Then, I'd make sure the staff knew exactly what I wanted them to do. I like to run a tight ship, so I'd make sure people show up early and are productive all day. Then, I'd make sure they finish all tasks before leaving for the day."

This approach is overly aggressive and would alienate employers. On the other end of the spectrum, here's another example of how *not* to answer this question.

"I'd want to get to know everyone in the office. It's important to have friends in the workplace, so I'd try to have coffee or lunch with each person individually.

"Then, I'd plan some team building activities. Maybe we could all go offsite to one of those company retreats. I think this would really help the staff get to know me."

While team building is important, so is getting work done. In your answers, you should find a balance between having an impact on the job and getting to know your co-workers.

Now, take a few minutes to go to the **Workbook Section** near the end of this book, and take notes on your ideas for these questions. Remember to focus on things that interest you and what you want from your next job.

Fit Questions

Fit Questions Overview

An interviewer might ask you a fit question, also known as a behavioral question, to see if you'd be a good fit in their company. Often, these questions start with, "Tell me about a time when . . ." or "How would you handle a situation if . . ." They want to know if your approach would be acceptable or compatible with the open role.

Here are a few popular fit questions:

- Tell me about a time when you . . .
  - demonstrated leadership
  - accomplished something you're proud of
  - had to deal with a difficult client
  - persuaded someone who didn't agree with you
  - used data to make a decision
  - developed a creative solution to a problem
- Tell me about a decision you regret.
- What's your greatest strength?
- What's your biggest weakness?

For these questions, you can use the S-T-A-R framework, which stands for Situation-Task-Action-Results. It's the easiest way to frame a clear, compelling response. Here's how it works:

S is for SITUATION:

Start with one sentence to describe the situation. This could be as simple as telling the interviewer where you were working and what your job title was. Here are examples:

A **graphic artist** could start with, "I was a freelance designer working on a project for a local smoothie shop."

A **sales person** might start with, "I was working at the Eastern University bookstore as a sales representative."

A **nurse** could begin, "When I was at Mercy Hospital, I was working as a staff nurse."

T is for TASK:

In one sentence, tell the interviewer what your assignment was.

The **graphic artist** could continue with, "My client wanted me to redesign their online menu."

The **sales person** could say, "My boss asked me to persuade the business school professors to recommend our store to their students."

The **nurse** might say, "Part of my job was to get a patient to take his medication, but that patient refused."

A is for ACTION:

In a few sentences, explain the specific actions you took to address the situation.

The **graphic artist** might continue, "I spent an afternoon at the smoothie shop, and I asked customers what they liked most about the place. They told me that they liked the cheerful atmosphere and fresh fruits that were used in the smoothies. Since that's what customers liked about the place, I designed the new online menu with bright, cheerful colors, and I included images of fresh fruit."

The **sales person** could say, "I hosted a free lunch for business school professors, and I asked them questions during that event. They told me that they were frustrated because their students would remember to buy textbooks, but they would forget to buy workbooks. I told the professors my bookstore would bundle the books for each class so students would automatically get all the books they needed. Then, I asked the professors to recommend my bookstore to their students."

The **nurse** could add, "I asked the patient what the problem was, and he told me that he didn't like the taste of the medicine. I noticed that he loved drinking apple juice, so I persuaded him to take the medicine, then quickly drink apple juice. I also told my supervisor about this approach."

R is for RESULTS:

Tell the interviewer about the results from your specific actions.

The **graphic artist** could conclude with, "Since the smoothie shop switched from their text-based online menu to my design with the bright colors and images of fresh fruits, their online orders have doubled."

The **sales person** could say, "The next semester, our sales of business books doubled because the professors told their students to get all the books they needed at our store."

Results for the **nurse** could be, "That patient began taking his medication every time he needed to, and we're now training our nurses to include juice chasers to help patients who don't like the taste of their medication."

You should have five or six stories prepared so you can answer a variety of fit questions. With the right stories, you can cover a broad range of questions. For example, you should have stories that can flex to address the following topics:

1. **Leadership** includes building a team, being persuasive, and getting results.

2. **Creativity** includes thinking outside the box and finding innovative solutions to challenging problems.

3. **Collaboration** includes building relationships and demonstrating interpersonal skills.

4. **Analytical skill** includes solving problems, thinking strategically, and applying mathematics to deliver results.

5. **Flexibility** includes being adaptable, prioritizing, and managing time effectively.

6. **Persistence** includes being focused, showing determination, and working hard.

For each of these categories, I've included an amazing answer that uses the S-T-A-R framework. You should customize a story for each of these, and you should be prepared to adapt your story to any variations in the interviewer's questions.

15. Demonstrate Leadership

When an interviewer asks you to tell them about a time when you demonstrated leadership, they want to hear that you can get people to follow you. This involves the ability to understand what motivates individuals and inspires their trust. It also involves the ability to communicate effectively in ways that get people to follow you.

You can use the same story, with minor modifications, for any of these variations:

Tell me about a time when you demonstrated:
- leadership
- persuasion
- teamwork

Here's an example that uses the S-T-A-R framework for a **shift manager** position at a restaurant. Responsibilities for this job might include leading the restaurant operations when the manager is not present, assigning tasks to employees, and resolving customer issues.

SITUATION: "When I was a cashier at the Big Burger Joint, two of our employees got into a shouting match."

TASK: "There wasn't a manager in the restaurant at the time, so I decided to address the issue."

ACTION: "I immediately told the two employees to come with me to the back office so they wouldn't continue to disrupt customers. Since I had good relationships with both employees, they complied. I got them to calm down and tell me the issue. I persuaded them to wait patiently while each of them told their side of the story. It turned out to be a misunderstanding as each thought the other had intentionally bumped into them. When they realized it was an accident because they were rushing to do the same task, they calmed down and agreed to go back to work. When the manager returned, I told her about the incident and let her know that it had been resolved."

RESULTS: "As a result, both employees learned to trust each other and give each other the benefit of the doubt. They've become good friends and work well together. Since I took the initiative to address the issue, I've been promoted to restaurant shift manager."

This example illustrates how a major component of leading is listening. An interviewer typically wants to hear that you can motivate people by listening to them and finding a solution that benefits them as well as the company. You should have a few S-T-A-R stories ready to show you can do this.

16. Demonstrate Creativity

For jobs that require out-of-the-box thinking, an interviewer wants to hear examples of how you've delivered creative solutions to challenging problems. They want you to give them an example of how you came up with an idea that no one else had thought of, and how that idea delivered results.

You should have at least one example that can answer any of the following variations of the creativity question:

Tell me about a time when you demonstrated:
- creativity
- out-of-the-box thinking
- an innovative approach

Here's an amazing answer using the S-T-A-R framework for a **public relations manager** position. Responsibilities for this job might include developing public relations strategy, writing press releases, and leading social media efforts.

SITUATION: "When I started working as the PR Coordinator at Middletown College Campus Theater, our attendance was extremely low."

TASK: "My job was to increase attendance at plays."

ACTION: "I looked at other entertainment businesses to see who did the best job of marketing. I noticed that movies generated most of their awareness using video trailers, so I thought that might work for our theater. I persuaded a friend, who was a visual arts major, to create a trailer for one of our plays as one of her class projects. I then ran that trailer on all the campus social media networks."

RESULTS: "The video trailers got over 2,000 views, and our attendance increased by more than 50%. When we surveyed attendees, more than 60% of them said that they first heard about the performances through the video trailers."

If you're in a creative field, but you don't have examples that demonstrate creativity, spend a few hours on a video site such as YouTube, Vimeo, or DailyMotion. Those sites feature creative ideas. For example, with a little research, you can learn how to create, publish, and promote videos about anything. A potential employer would be impressed if you told them that you've posted tutorials for a topic that interests you, which could include anything from driving awareness for a charitable organization to tutoring kids on math problems.

17. Demonstrate Collaboration

Many jobs require that you work well with others, so an interviewer might want you to demonstrate that skill. Here are variations of the collaboration question:

Tell me about a time when you demonstrated:
- collaboration
- interpersonal skills
- ability to work with challenging people

Here's an amazing answer using the S-T-A-R framework for a **computer programmer** position. Responsibilities for this job might include writing code for computer applications and integrating work with coding from other programmers.

SITUATION: "I was working as a programmer on a new video game for Pixelation Gaming Company."

TASK: "My job was to write the code for the vehicles in the game."

ACTION: "About half way through the project, the creative director and the project manager couldn't agree on an ending for the game. I had a good relationship with both of them, so I persuaded them to have a war room session with me. During that session, I facilitated a brainstorming exercise for them to voice their ideas. We came up with several ideas that we hadn't previously considered, and one of those ideas was the option we decided to go with."

RESULTS: "The result was that we were able to agree on a solution that we all liked, and the project was completed on time. That game has become a best seller for the company."

For collaboration questions, the interviewer wants to see that you can get people to work toward a common objective. They want to see that you can listen to multiple points of view and find common ground.

18. Demonstrate Analytical Skills

If you're interviewing for a job that requires analytical skills, the interviewer will want to hear how you use data to make decisions. Here are variations of the analytical question:

Tell me about a time when you demonstrated:
- analytical skills
- an ability to solve complex problems
- an ability to think strategically
- an ability to use data to make a decision

Here's an amazing answer using the S-T-A-R framework for an **innovation director** at a sporting goods company.

Responsibilities for this job might include identifying new product lines and determining market potential for new items.

SITUATION: "I was working as an innovation manager for Premier Sporting Goods."

TASK: "My job was to identify and assess business opportunities for new lines of sports equipment."

ACTION: "When I was at my son's martial arts tournament, I noticed hundreds of kids with sparring gear, so I looked into that as a potential new product line. In my research, I learned that over 4 million Americans participate in some form of marital arts. Participants spend an average of $200 annually on gear. That translates into an $800 million retail opportunity. With an average mark-up of 50%, the wholesale opportunity is around $400 million. I used this information to persuade our executive team to approve a test market for a new line of martial arts gear."

RESULTS: "The result was that we created a new product line that is now delivering over $4 million in sales annually. With only a 1% market share, there's plenty of room to grow that business."

For analytical questions, the interviewer wants to see that you can find relevant data and use it to make informed decisions. They want to see that you can conduct research and make realistic assumptions as needed.

19. Demonstrate Flexibility

An interviewer might want to hear how you deal with challenging situations. They may be looking for someone who can manage competing priorities and work on ambiguous projects.

Here are variations on the flexibility questions that they may ask:

Tell me about a time when you demonstrated:
- flexibility
- an ability to prioritize
- time management skills

Here's an amazing answer using the S-T-A-R framework for a **civil engineer**. Responsibilities for this job could include planning construction projects for commercial buildings and monitoring progress on projects.

SITUATION: "I was working as a civil engineer for JCN Construction Company."

TASK: "I had three projects happening at the same time, and all three project managers wanted me to work full-time on their projects."

ACTIONS: "I met with each manager to go through the project timelines to see what work was most urgent. I noticed that materials for one project wouldn't arrive at the construction site for another six months, so I persuaded that manager to move his timelines out a few weeks. For another project, I could delegate some of my drafting tasks to a junior team member. Then, I focused my efforts on the most urgent project with the tasks that only I could do. I also followed up with the junior person to ensure that they were progressing on their tasks. When those projects were complete, I focused on the third project that was less urgent."

RESULTS: "By prioritizing and delegating, I was able to complete all three projects on time. One project even came in under budget because I was able to delegate work to someone who had a lower billing rate."

Interviewers love to see a candidate who knows how to prioritize. They also want to see someone who can keep managers informed as they make decisions about the work. Craft your answers related to flexibility, prioritization, and time management to demonstrate you skills while ensuring your manager agrees with your approach.

20. Demonstrate Persistence

Interviewers love to find candidates who show that they can work hard and be persistent about challenging problems. To assess this, an interviewer might ask you any of the following variations of the persistence question:

Tell me about a time when you demonstrated:
- persistence
- an ability to address a challenging situation
- a willingness to go the extra mile
- a strong work ethic

Here's an amazing answer for any of these questions for someone applying to be a **physician assistant**. Responsibilities for this job might include interviewing patients, performing physical examinations, and consulting with physicians on the treatment of medical conditions.

SITUATION: "I was working as a Physician's Assistant at the Cleveland Clinic."

TASK: "I had a patient who had come into our clinic with a rash on her shoulder. She said she had seen four doctors, including two allergy specialists, and none of them gave her a treatment that worked."

ACTION: "I met with the patient, took a full medical history, and asked her about her work and home environment. I then researched the possible causes for that type of rash. I also interviewed her daughter, who had recently visited Madagascar. I found an article about a rare allergic reaction that is triggered by fabric made from a plant in Madagascar. I then referred the patient to a doctor who specialized in rare allergic reactions. He confirmed that her reaction was from a shirt brought by the patient's daughter from Madagascar."

RESULTS: "By conducting a thorough patient assessment and extensive research, I diagnosed something that four physicians had missed. I love solving problems, and I'll do whatever I can to learn the cause of my patients' medical issues."

Interviewers want to know that you'll go the extra mile to get your work done. By having an answer like the one above, you'll set yourself apart from other candidates.

21. A Decision You Regretted

An interviewer might ask you about a decision that you regret to determine if you learn from your mistakes. Such questions allow you to show your ability to adapt and use your experience to be more effective.

With this type question, give an example that highlights a key skill from the job description. That way, the interviewer will see that you learned from your previous experience, and you're less likely to make the same mistake if you are hired.

Here's a strong answer for someone applying to be a **strategy director**. Responsibilities for this job might include leading strategic projects, managing teams of external consultants, and developing recommendations for new business models to present to company executives.

SITUATION: "I was working as a strategy manager at Miser Bank."

TASK: "My assignment was to write a project brief to prepare our consulting company for an upcoming project. The project involved developing a new strategy for improving our customer satisfaction."

ACTION: "I wrote the brief using a template that our bank had used for consulting projects in the past."

RESULTS: "The consulting firm assigned a team with financial experts, but they didn't include anyone with customer research experience. As a result, their initial recommendations primarily involved cost-cutting measures, but their recommendations didn't address our primary objective, which was to improve customer satisfaction.

"I realized that the consultants needed to approach the project from a different angle, so I met with their project leader. I asked her to help me re-write the project brief so it would identify the skills needed for the specific assignment.

"Because I identified my mistake early in the process, I was able to get the consulting firm to assign someone with the expertise needed for the project. Also, I revised the company's project brief template to include "specific skills needed" so we wouldn't repeat this issue on future projects. The bank's financial team estimated that the new brief will save the company approximately $100,000 per year in consulting fees because projects would always include consultants with the specific skills needed.

"From that experience, I learned that each project is unique, and I need to evaluate each project's scope to ensure I get team members with the right skills to address the specific needs of the project."

This is an amazing answer because the candidate demonstrated how they learned from a mistake and found a way to prevent others from making the same mistake.

When preparing for this question, use an example that highlights how you can improve the company once you are hired. The interviewer will see you as an amazing choice because you did not simply make a mistake and move on. You learned and helped others to avoid making the same mistake.

22. Address Competing Priorities

This is a great question to see if a candidate can prioritize a challenging workload. With this question, an interviewer wants to hear if you make good choices and keep supervisors informed when you have to make trade-offs.

When I ask this question, I like to hear how a candidate can delegate work when possible, or how they decide which projects require immediate attention and which can be deferred. Here's an amazing answer to this question for someone applying to be an **administrative assistant.** Responsibilities for this position might include scheduling appointments, preparing expense reports, and performing other administrative tasks.

SITUATION: "In my current job, I support our company's Vice President of Sales."

TASK: "Last month, I was preparing for our national sales meeting, and my boss had an urgent request from our Chief Executive Officer to host a market tour for one of our board members."

ACTION: "I immediately contacted three of our regional

sales directors to see if one of them could host the market tour. One person was excited about the opportunity, so I delegated the planning to him. I asked the CEO's administrative assistant to work directly with the regional sales director on the marketing tour details, and they copied me on their plans so I could keep my boss informed.

"For the national sales meeting, I enlisted the help of a sales analyst who had an interest in meeting planning. She helped me identify the venue, manage the attendee list, and coordinate the presentations.

"Throughout the process, I sent my boss daily updates regarding the market tour and the national meeting."

RESULTS: "Because I was able to delegate the work for these two complex projects to team members who were excited about the work, both projects were incredibly successful. We sent surveys to the attendees, and they rated it as the best sales meeting that we've hosted during the past 10 years.

"After the market tour, the board member sent our CEO a glowing note of appreciation. The CEO said that market tour was one reason that he promoted my boss to Senior VP of Sales and Marketing. I am proud of this accomplishment because I love seeing a promotion happen for someone I support."

I love the way this candidate concluded the answer. It's a nice touch to tell your interviewer that you're happy to help your boss get promoted. Since they may be your boss, they will make the connection that you can help them move up in the company.

This answer shows the candidate's flexibility. Employers like employees who can adapt to changing circumstances by finding other people in the organization who can help with projects.

23. Your Greatest Strength

This should be one of the easiest questions in an interview, but I've seen candidates give answers that had nothing to do with the roles they were interviewing for. I've also seen candidates give a brief answer without connecting it to the job they want. For example, when I've interviewed for marketing roles, candidates have told me that their greatest strength is organization. While this is a great answer for an accountant, it's not a great answer for an aspiring marketer.

You should answer this question with a strength that directly relates to the role; then follow up with an example of using that strength to get results. Here are examples of strengths that directly relate to specific jobs:

- Accountant → attention to detail
- Manager → ability to lead people
- Sales person → ability to build strong relationships
- Doctor → ability to diagnose and treat complex conditions

When answering this question, go with the strengths that will make you effective in your next role. Then, follow it up with a clear example of how you've used that strength to get impressive results in the past.

Here's an amazing example for someone applying to be a **psychiatrist**. Responsibilities for this job might include diagnosing and treating patients who have cognitive or emotional challenges.

SITUATION: "I've always been a great listener. During my residency, my supervisors consistently rated my ability as exceptional when it came to listening to patients and discovering important details that others had missed."

TASK: "One time, my supervisor asked me to conduct an interview with a woman who had been diagnosed with obsessive compulsive disorder to determine the best course of treatment."

ACTION: "During the interview, the woman casually mentioned that she had a difficult time in high school. I asked her a series of questions to get details. Eventually, I was able get her to reveal that she saw one of her close friends get seriously injured in an accident. I determined that her symptoms began shortly after that incident. With this information, I was able to correct her diagnosis from OCD to post-traumatic stress disorder."

RESULTS: "Because I listened carefully and caught a detail that others had missed, I was able to re-diagnose a woman who was incorrectly diagnosed for years. As a result, our treatment team was able to get her on the proper medication, and she's been able to hold down a job, get re-married to her husband, and return to being a good mother."

Your interviewer wants you to tell them about a strength that will make you an exceptional employee. As such, when you review the job description, think about what you do exceptionally well that matches the skills they need. Then, tell your best example of how you've leveraged that skill to get results in the past.

24. Your Biggest Weakness

Interviewers might ask this question to see how self-aware you are. If you say you have no weaknesses, they might see you as arrogant and difficult to work with. If you tell them about a weakness that is really a strength, they might see you as insincere.

I recommend you answer this question with either a weakness that you've overcome or a weakness that has nothing to do with the role that you're interviewing for.

Here's an example for a **sales vice president** position. Responsibilities for this job could include leading sales strategy for a department, determining recruiting and training needs, and making changes to department's organizational structure as needed.

SITUATION: "I've always been better at focusing on the big picture than on details. When I started my career as a sales person, that issue created challenges for me."

TASK: "For example, I was assigned to sell our complex line of pet food to a major retailer, and they wanted exclusive pricing deals for every item we sold them."

ACTION: "I tried to manage the complex details of their pricing plan, and it was difficult for me to get every detail right. Fortunately, I learned to get my finance counterparts involved in transactions that required detailed attention."

RESULTS: "Through that experience, I've learned to build relationships with people who are strong in areas where I'm not. My finance counterparts are some of my most valued colleagues. They value my ability to build customer relationships and develop effective sales strategies, and I value their ability to manage the details. As a result, my team has led our company in sales for the past three years."

I love this example because it shows that the candidate can be effective in the specific role they're interviewing for. A Sales Vice President shouldn't be involved in details, so it's acceptable that they're not a detailed person. However, they need to recognize their weakness and plan to compensate for it.

If you're asked about your biggest weakness, give an

honest answer, but give an answer that still makes you a good choice for the specific job you're interviewing for. Also, show how you've learned to compensate for your weakness, either by leveraging other people or developing a process to overcome your challenge.

25. Your Tolerance for Risk

An interviewer may ask this question to see if your risk tolerance is consistent with the company's culture. Your answer should depend on how your potential employer views risk.

In some industries, such as high-tech, risk is encouraged as part of the development process. In other industries, such as the medical field, risk may be discouraged at all cost.

Here are amazing answers for a **computer software developer** whose responsibilities might include designing computer game applications, testing software, and implementing patches.

SITUATION: "I enjoy taking risks. It helps me learn and expand my skills. For example, a few years ago I was working on a new first-person-shooter game."

TASK: "My job was to design weapons for the game."

ACTION: "The original project specs called for standard weapons like traditional pistols and rifles. I thought it would be interesting to see if I could develop weapons with bullets that exploded on impact.

"I spent a few days researching the coding that was used in racing games to show explosions when cars crashed. After a few failed attempts, I found a way to replicate those special effects in the first-person-shooter environment."

RESULTS: "The result was a weapon that we called *the*

zombie killer, and its intense explosion effect surpassed any weapon in shooter games. In fact, when the game was reviewed by *Gamer Magazine*, they credited that weapon as one of the main reasons they rated the game as Top First-Person-Shooter of the year."

Now, compare that answer with the following response for a job in a risk-averse industry. This is how a **pharmacist** might answer when their responsibilities include filling prescriptions, verifying physician instructions, and instructing patients on use of prescribed medicine.

SITUATION: "I am very careful to avoid taking risks. In the pharmacy business, risks can have life or death consequences. For example, a few years ago, I was doing my residency in a small, rural pharmacy."

TASK: "Part of my job was to double-check prescriptions to reduce the risk of adverse drug interactions."

ACTION: "Since that pharmacy didn't have an automated system for detecting drug interactions, I offered to find a software program that would help.

"I conducted extensive research to identify the most trusted software available. When I found the most respected software, I developed a beta test to ensure the software worked properly on our computer systems. For six months, we checked to see that the software detected adverse reactions on every prescription we filled.

"During that beta test, I noticed that the software didn't work properly on our old computer systems. I persuaded the pharmacy owner to invest in new computers so our software would work properly. I then completed the beta test and ensured that the software was effective for detecting adverse drug combinations."

RESULTS: "Near the end of my residency, that pharmacy underwent a thorough audit, in which the FDA reviewed our prescriptions for the past three years. They discovered that after we implemented the software, the number of potentially harmful drug combinations in our prescriptions decreased by over 80%. Because I was so careful, that pharmacy was able to make prescriptions safer for our customers."

As you can see, your answer to this question should be tailored to the role you want. In your research, you should see if risks are encouraged in your field. You should also see if anyone in the company can give you an indication of how risks are perceived there.

If the company's culture encourages taking risks and you enjoy risks, say so. If the company discourages risks and you are a careful person, say so. If your risk tolerance doesn't align with that of the company, you may want to pass on the opportunity and find another company that's a better fit for you. Nothing is more frustrating that working somewhere that isn't a good fit for you.

26. Your Friends' Description of You

This is a great opportunity for you to highlight some of your best attributes. As always, include details that demonstrate your ability to be effective in the job you're applying for.

Think about the people you work closely with, and think about how they would describe you. What are the characteristics that they would say make you effective at your job? Are you friendly, inspiring, collaborative, creative, or a great listener? Now, pick a relevant characteristic for your career goals, and tell a story that illustrates your ability to use that characteristic to get results.

Here's an example for someone applying to be a **radio talk show host**. Responsibilities for this job might include announcing radio station programming, commenting on current events, interviewing guests, and entertaining an audience.

SITUATION: "My friends would describe me as entertaining… maybe as the life of the party. When I was in college, I was telling stories to a few friends over lunch."

TASK: "One of my friends dared me to record the story on a video and post it to social media."

ACTION: "I took the dare, created the video, and posted it on Facebook. Within days, my video got over 1,000 views. I then posted the video on YouTube and created my own YouTube channel. Now, every time I come up with a story, I record it on video and upload it to my YouTube Channel."

RESULTS: "As a result, I now have over 10,000 subscribers to my channel, and my videos have gotten over 1,000,000 views. I'd like to use my ability to entertain people to be a sports reporter. I love sports and I love entertaining people. Since my friends and my YouTube audience say I'm good at it, I'm here with you to see if we can make it happen. If you want to see if my friends are right, I invite you to check my YouTube videos and decide for yourself."

While being described as *entertaining* wouldn't be a good answer for most jobs, it's perfect for a role in the entertainment industry. When you prepare for this question, pick a relevant characteristic for the role you want, and tell a compelling story about how you've leveraged that characteristic to get results.

Fit Questions: Dos and Don'ts

With fit questions, most interviewers appreciate real-life stories. Those stories give them confidence you can assess challenging situations and take the actions needed to get results. Here are a few dos and don'ts for fit questions.

Do:
- Have five or six stories ready to go. That way, you can answer a variety of fit questions.
- Use the S-T-A-R framework.
- Limit your S, T, and R to one or two sentences each. The interviewer wants to see that you can communicate succinctly, so spend your time on your actions, not the other aspects of your story.
- Be specific about your actions. Tell the interviewer exactly what you did personally.
- Make sure your results are clear and compelling. Always end your story with positive results. Interviewers are looking for problem solvers, so compelling results are a must. If you didn't get a positive result, use a different story.

Don't:
- Don't ramble. Interviewers will lose interest if you take too long to get to the point.
- Don't be negative. No matter how bad the situation was, you need to show that you got to a positive outcome.

For reference, here is an example of how not to answer a Fit question like, "Tell me about a time when you demonstrated leadership." This example is for a **shift manager** at a fast food restaurant. Responsibilities for this job might include leading the restaurant operations when the manager is not present, assigning tasks to employees, and resolving customer issues.

"I've always been a great basketball player. When I was in high school, I led my team in points per game and rebounds.

"I also once led a group of fellow Boy Scouts on a hike. We went to a beautiful national park, and I was the fastest hiker in the group. I was so fast that the other kids had a difficult time keeping up with me.

"Another time, I led the debate team with the highest number of wins in debate competitions. I'm very competitive, so I worked hard at beating out my team member. If you hire me, I'll bring that competitive spirit, and I'll find a way to beat my co-workers at any goals you set for me."

First, this candidate is rambling on with multiple examples that have nothing to do with the open role. A good answer to this question would focus on one example that shows how the candidate can effectively motivate others to follow him.

Also, the candidate doesn't seem to understand leadership. Rather than talking about being better than team members, he should focus on how he built a team that has successfully accomplished a goal. That way, the interviewer could see him as someone who could lead a shift of workers at a restaurant.

Now, take a few minutes to go to the **Workbook Section** near the end of this book, and start taking notes on your ideas for these questions. Remember to briefly explain the Situation and the Tasks you were assigned. Then, clearly state the specific Actions you took and the Results.

Case Questions

Case Questions Overview

With case questions, interviewers typically ask you to explain how you would approach specific situations related to the job. With these questions, interviewers might want you to demonstrate how you would address a hypothetical situation like a business emergency or an opportunity that arises with a customer. They might also ask you to formulate a recommendation, to assess a sample of someone's work, or make a persuasive argument.

Here are common examples of case questions:

Sales Jobs:	"Persuade me to buy this pen from you."
Analytical Jobs:	"How many golf balls could fit in this room?"
Logistics Jobs:	"What would you do if a natural disaster wiped out your only distribution road?"
Marketing Jobs:	"What is your favorite marketing campaign, and why?"
General Manager:	"If I asked you to open a new business, how would you approach that?"
Medical Jobs:	"If you had a patient who was crashing, what would you do?"

Interviewers typically ask case questions to test your problem-solving abilities or specific job skills.

I recommend you start formulating your answer by requesting more information about the situation. Ask a few clarifying questions. This will show that you can assess a situation before jumping to a conclusion. It will also buy you some time to think about your response.

You should also state your assumptions as well as your criteria for your recommendations. For example, for the question about your favorite medication, start by saying that your choice is based on criteria such as effectiveness in treating a significant medical condition, absence of major adverse side effects, and reasonable price. The interviewer will see that you can formulate recommendations based on relevant criteria.

Here are examples of common case questions along with a few amazing answers.

27. Persuade Me to . . .

"Persuade me to buy your pen from you," is a common interview question for sales jobs. Versions of this question for other jobs could include, "Persuade me to take my medication" in the healthcare field and, "Persuade me to learn a complex concept if I'm an unwilling student" in the academic field. Employers use questions like these to see if candidates can be persuasive.

Rather than jumping in with the benefits of a specific pen, medication, or academic concept, I prefer to hear candidates ask a few questions first. Often, the best way to persuade someone is to learn what motivates them, and then craft your persuasive argument accordingly. That way, you're focusing on benefits that appeal to them, not things that you think are important.

Here is the most amazing answer I've ever heard for the "Persuade me to buy your pen" question. This example is for a **salesperson** position with responsibilities that include greeting customers, processing sales transactions, and answering customer questions.

Interviewer: "Persuade me to buy your pen."

Candidate: "When was the last time you used a pen?"

Interviewer: "I haven't used a pen in years. I've gone completely paperless so I don't need pens."

Candidate: "Hmm. Do you have kids?"

Interviewer: "Yes, I have a six-year-old daughter."

Candidate: "Does she read?"

Interviewer: "Yes."

Candidate: "Does she use e-mail?"

Interviewer: "Of course not. She's only six."

Candidate: "Do you travel for work?"

Interviewer: "Yes, I travel on a regular basis."

Candidate: "Do you have any long trips coming up?"

Interviewer: "Yes, next month, I have a business trip to China, and I'll be gone for two weeks."

Candidate: "Does your daughter miss you when you're gone?"

Interviewer: "Yes, but what does that have to do with this pen."

Candidate: "Well, here's my sales pitch. Imagine your daughter is missing you when you've been gone for over a week. You could send her an e-mail, but she doesn't use email. Even if you could get an e-mail to her, that might seem a bit impersonal. You could call her, but that phone call would last only a few minutes.

"Imagine you leave a nice, handwritten letter that she can read while you're gone. She could pull out that letter and read it when she is missing you. She could show that letter to her friends and let them know how much her dad cares about her. She could save that letter for years, looking back at it anytime she wants to be reminded that you think about her even when you're not there.

"Someday, when she has kids of her own, she can show the letter to them, and she can tell them what a caring person their grandfather is.

"Now, I know it might be difficult to write a heartfelt letter to your daughter, so here's what I'm going to do. If you buy this pen from me today, I'll help you craft a message that she'll treasure for years to come. You see, I leave notes for my son every time I travel for more than a few days, so I have a lot of practice at this. I bet that you and I could come up with an amazing letter that your daughter will absolutely love.

"So what do you say? Will you buy this pen from me so we can get started on that letter?"

I love this answer because it shows the candidate can think beyond the obvious benefits of a pen. It taps into an emotional need that the interviewer has to connect with his daughter. By asking a few questions before crafting the sales pitch, the interviewer came up with a personalized benefit that was far more persuasive than a generic sales pitch.

If an interviewer asks you to make a persuasive argument, ask a few questions first. That way, you can frame your response in a way that taps into a benefit that's important to them. That will show that you're an expert in persuasion.

28. Estimate the Number of . . .

An interviewer might want to test your analytical skills, so you might get a question like, "Estimate the number of golf balls that would fit in this room." Variations of this question could include, "Estimate the number of chairs in this city," or "Estimate the number of bricks you'd need to cover the exterior of this building."

Typically, interviewers don't expect you to get the correct answer. In fact, they probably don't even know the correct answer. They want to see how good you are at thinking under pressure and making assumptions when addressing a problem.

Please don't give an answer like, "I don't know . . . maybe a million." That doesn't tell the interviewer anything about you. Instead, make some assumptions and make some estimates. That way, the interviewer can follow your thought process.

Here's how you could approach the golf ball question if you were a **data analyst**. Responsibilities for a job like this could include analyzing data, evaluating financial information, and preparing recommendations for improving business results.

Interviewer: "How many golf balls would fit in this room?"

Candidate: "First, I'd have to know how big the golf balls are. Can I look up that information, or do you want me to make an assumption?"

Interviewer: "I'd like you to make assumptions. Don't look up anything. I'm not looking for the right answer. I just want to see how you think."

Candidate: "Okay. I'll assume the golf balls are between one and two inches in diameter. For this exercise, let's say they're 1.5 inches. Then, I'd want to know how many balls would be in a line that's one foot long. So, two balls would be three inches long, four balls would be six inches long, and eight balls would be twelve inches long. Do you mind if I take some notes?"

Interviewer: "Go right ahead."

Candidate: "Okay. I'll write down eight golf balls per linear foot. That means there are eight times eight balls in a square foot. That's 64. For a cubic foot, I'll need to multiple that by eight balls high. Eight times 64 is, let's see, according to my math, that's 512. I'll round that down to 500 to make the math easier. How am I doing so far?"

Interviewer: "Good. Keep going."

Candidate: "Next, I'll need to know how many cubic feet are in this room. I notice the ceiling tiles look to be about one foot by one foot. I count ten tiles along the length of the room, times ten tiles across the width. That means the room is about 100 square feet. The ceiling is high. I'd say it's about ten feet high. That would mean there are 1,000 cubic feet in this room. So, if I filled the room with golf balls, it would take 500 balls per cubic foot times 1,000 cubic feet. That would be about 500,000 golf balls."

Interviewer: "Okay. Now, tell me what factors might cause that number to be incorrect."

Candidate: "Hmm. Well, golf balls aren't perfect cubes. They're spheres. That means they'll settle a bit, so there are probably more than 500 golf balls in a cubic foot. Also, I assumed the room would be empty. Since there are two chairs, a desk, and two people, we can't put golf balls into that space. If you factor in the settling and the space we're taking up, I think they'd cancel each other out. If I have the size of the golf balls right, I'll stick with my answer of 500,000."

If you're looking for a job that requires computation or analytical skills, you might want to practice a few estimation questions. Since there's no way to predict the exact question you might be asked, just run through a few of these scenarios:

- How many trees are there in a square mile of forest?
- How many blades of grass are on a football field?
- How many cars would fit inside one square mile?

29. What's Your Favorite…

An interviewer might ask you to pick a favorite thing related to your industry. For marketers, it could be your favorite advertising campaign. For someone in the medical field, it could be your favorite medication. For someone in construction, it could be your favorite power tool. For a teacher, it could be your favorite teaching technique.

The interviewer wants you to show that you can evaluate your choice based on its ability to accomplish a strategic objective. For this question, you'll want to state your answer and your criteria for selecting your favorite thing. Then, explain how your favorite thing delivers on those criteria.

Here's an example of an amazing answer for a question like "What's your favorite advertising campaign?" for someone applying for a **marketing manager** position. Responsibilities for this role might include manage a team of marketing staff, developing advertising strategies, and evaluating marketing campaign elements.

"My favorite campaign is the Super Fresh toothpaste campaign. Here's the criteria I'll use to show why this is a great campaign. First, to be effective, a campaign should differentiate the brand from its competitors with a benefit that the target audience cares about. Second, it should break through the clutter in the media environment. And third, it should deliver results.

"When the campaign started, Super Fresh had less than 5% market share in the toothpaste category. While other brands were focusing on whitening as their benefit, Super Fresh focused on fresh breath. I read an article about the campaign that said 30% of consumers picked fresh breath as the benefit that was most important to them. Among Super Fresh's primary target, which was young men, over 40% picked fresh breath as their top priority for toothpaste. That seems like a relevant benefit for Super Fresh's target audience.

"Next, the Super Fresh ads did an amazing job of breaking through. The ads used impressive special effects to show animated stinky guys appearing around teeth. When a giant toothbrush with Super Fresh toothpaste slid across the teeth, the animated stinky guys ran away, and clean, shiny teeth remained. The visuals were clear and impressive.

"Finally, in the first two years of the campaign, Super Fresh market share grew from 5% to 8%. Among their primary target audience, their share grew from 6% to 12%.

"To summarize, my favorite campaign is the Super Fresh campaign because it communicated a relevant benefit, it broke through in a cluttered media environment, and it delivered results."

If you're interviewing for business jobs, you should prepare for questions about your favorite advertising campaign, product launch, business strategy, or similar situation. I recommend you list your criteria before explaining your selection. That way, an interviewer can see that you're able to make decisions based on criteria that are strategically relevant for a business or a brand.

This approach can work for questions in other career fields. For example, if you're interviewing for a job in the medical field, you may be asked about your favorite medication, your favorite approach to calming an anxious patient, or your favorite hospital. You can use the approach above to outline your criteria, and then explain how your selection delivers on those criteria.

30. A Disaster

An interviewer might ask how you would approach a hypothetical situation to test your problem-solving abilities. One of my favorite such questions follows: "A storm wiped out the only bridge to your only warehouse which is located on an island. You can't get your products to market. What do you do?"

Here's an amazing answer to this question for someone applying for a job as a **logistics manager**. Responsibilities for that position might include determining the most efficient methods for transporting goods, identifying ways to increase speed of delivery, and addressing logistical issues as they arise.

"First, I would contact the warehouse manager to make sure all the employees and their family members were okay. If everyone wasn't okay or if people were still in danger, I would focus my efforts on their safety.

"I'll assume that everyone was okay. Next, I'd call an emergency meeting of the smartest people I know to gather a variety of suggestions. I'd want to include people from Operations, Engineering, R&D, Design, and other functions to help develop solutions. I'd get their help to identify and execute the best possible solution.

"I'd focus on gathering as much information as possible. I'd need to know exactly what I'm solving. For example, I'd want to know how far the warehouse was from a working road system or railway, and I'd want to know exactly what obstacles were in the way. For example, was I dealing with a giant canyon, a rushing river, or a calm lake?

"I'd also want to know the value, density, and perishability of the inventory. And I'd want to know the urgency of any commitments to deliver inventory to customers.

If I was in danger of missing delivery deadlines, I'd contact my customers immediately to explain the situation. I'd work with them to see if I could delay the delivery dates as needed.

"Then, I'd see if my company had assets that could transport the inventory to the mainland. For example, if I had to get the inventory across a calm lake, does my company have amphibious vehicles? If so, I would see if I could use them to get the inventory across the lake to a road on the mainland.

"If my company didn't have an in-house solution, I'd start calling companies that specialize in moving inventory across water. In evaluating those companies, I'd consider density and value of the inventory. If it consists of small, lightweight items like precious gems or high-value computer chips, I'd consider hiring a helicopter to fly to the warehouse and move the inventory to the mainland.

"If the inventory was heavy or bulky, I'd start looking for companies that could provide temporary bridges or barges that could transport heavy items.

"Do you want me to keep going, or is that enough information?"

This answer demonstrates an ability to evaluate a situation and generate solutions based on specific circumstances. I like the answer because it starts by focusing on the safety of the company's employees. By doing that, this candidate shows compassion for fellow employees.

Then, the answer demonstrates that the candidate is willing to involve others in the problem-solving process. An interviewer will appreciate that the candidate doesn't rely only on himself or herself to solve challenging problems.

Next, the candidate demonstrates an ability to develop a variety of solutions that factor into circumstances such as urgency, potential obstacles, and cost implications.

31. Open a New Business

One of my favorite case questions is "If I hired you to open a new business, how would you approach that?" This helps me determine whether a candidate understands the key factors that lead to business success.

To answer questions like these, I recommend that you use a framework like the 4 Cs. The first C is COMPANY. What resources does your company have? Do you have any industry experts, patents, brands, or production capabilities that you can leverage?

The second C is CUSTOMER. What are your potential customers looking for? What are their unmet needs or their areas of dissatisfaction?

The third C is COMPETITION. Who are your competitors? What are their strengths and weaknesses? What can you deliver that they can't?

The final C is CONCLUSION. How do you assess the first three Cs to form your recommendation?

Here's an example of a great response for someone applying for a **general manager** position. Responsibilities for the job could include defining the priorities of an organization, overseeing the organization's staffing activities, and evaluating key projects and investments.

COMPANY: "First, I'd want to know what resources I have to start the business. For example, do I have access to people with expertise in a particular type of business? Do I have adequate funds to pay initial start-up costs? Do I have production capabilities that I can leverage?"

CUSTOMER: "Next, I'd want to know as much as possible about my potential customers. I'd want to know about trends that I could tap into. I'd also want to know if customers are looking for benefits that aren't currently being addressed. As I learned about potential customers, I'd look for underserved segments that I could target."

COMPETITION: "I'd also want to know as much as possible about my potential competition. Are there any big, entrenched competitors that have a stronger brand or more resources than I do? I'd want to know about potential barriers to entering the business so I could anticipate the future competitive environment."

CONCLUSION: "Finally, based on my company's resources, the needs of potential customers, and the competitive environment, I'd prepare a SWOT analysis. I'd list my Strengths and Weaknesses based on the competitive set. I'd also list the Opportunities and Threats that are present with potential customers and competitors. That would help me select a business strategy that would lead to success."

A framework like the 4 Cs will help you organize your answer so the interviewer will see you as a clear communicator with strong strategic skills. Too often, candidates will list their business ideas and neglect their approach.

Interviewers typically aren't looking for your ability to generate ideas. They're looking for your ability to think logically and make recommendations based on relevant criteria.

32. Declining Sales

Another common case question is: "Your company's sales are declining. How would you address the issue?" For this question, you can also use the 4 Cs framework.

Here's an example of a good answer for someone

applying to a **finance manager** position. Responsibilities for that job could include analyzing financial information, and preparing recommendations for allocating budgets and improving investment returns

COMPANY: "First, I'd look internally to see if we're doing something wrong. I'd see if our product quality is declining. Then, I'd see if we have cut back on our advertising or changed our pricing strategy."

CUSTOMERS: "Next, I'd see what is happening with our customers. I'd want to see if our sales are declining across all customers or if a few customers are responsible for the declines. Once I see which customers are declining, I'd contact them to see why they aren't buying as much."

COMPETITION: "I'd also want to know what is happening with my competitors. I'd see if they have launched new products, if they changed pricing, or if they've had a new advertising campaign."

CONCLUSION: "I'd use this information to see if I need to make any changes to my product portfolio. I might need innovation to address changing customer needs or to get ahead of competitors. I might also need to change my pricing approach or distribution strategy. I'd also consider launching a new advertising campaign."

Using a framework like the 4 Cs demonstrates that you can look at challenging situations from multiple angles. Too often, a candidate will jump to a single answer like lowering price or launching a new product.

I like the answer above because the candidate explained that they'd gather information, assess that information, and formulate a recommendation based on the specific business situation. This approach will differentiate you from other candidates whose responses don't show your thoughtfulness.

33. Double Your Money

One of my favorite case questions is, "If I gave you $100, what could you do to double it in the next four hours?" This is another great question for determining if a candidate can think on their feet and make good business decisions. It also shows if a candidate can develop creative solutions that deliver business benefits.

The 4 Cs framework can be effective for questions like this. Here's how it could be used for someone applying for a job as an **accountant**. Responsibilities for that job might include organizing financial records, recommending improvements to business processes, and identifying ways to increase revenue and reduce costs.

COMPANY: "I'd want to know about available resources. For example, I have a car, there's a grocery store nearby, and I'm in a big city full of potential customers."

CUSTOMERS: "Next, I'd think about the customer needs that I can address. Since it's summertime now, I might be able to leverage that to my advantage. It's also especially hot and dry today. There are a few nearby places where I could find big groups of thirsty customers that I could sell beverages to.

"I noticed there's a big construction site down the street, there's a festival at the city park this afternoon, and there's a lot of people walking around in the downtown area. Looking at those three groups, I'd want to pick the group that would be willing to pay the most for a beverage that I could offer. I might go with the festival crowd since they're the most likely to have spending money."

COMPETITION: "I'd also want to know who my competitors are. If the festival is a beer festival, it's not likely that I can sell many beverages because there will be too much competition. If it's a chili cook-off, there may be less competition. There also might be high demand for beverages because people are tasting chili, and nothing goes better with chili than a cold, refreshing beverage."

CONCLUSION: "Assuming I could sell beverages legally at the festival and the competition is minimal, I'd look into the cost and revenue potential. I could buy bottled water by the case that the grocery store sells for around 20¢ per bottle. I could also buy a few cheap coolers for around $20 and a few bags of ice for another $20. That would leave me $60 for bottled water, so I could have 300 bottles. If I sold them for $1 each, I'd generate $300 in revenue. After I paid my costs, that would give me $200 in profit, exactly enough to double your money. How's that?"

I'll tell you how that is… amazing! This candidate talked herself into a job. She showed that she could assess a challenging business situation, make a few calculated assumptions, and generate exactly enough revenue to address the specific objective.

Now, think about the types of situations you might encounter in your desired job. Then think about the criteria you would use or the information you would want to address in those situations. If you explain your assumptions and show your logic, an interviewer will be impressed. They will also give you more credit for your recommendation if you demonstrate your thought process in your answer.

Case Questions: Dos and Don'ts

With case questions, interviewers want to see that you can think through challenging problems or address situations that might arise in the job they're trying to fill. Here are a few tips for case questions.

Do:
- Ask a few clarifying questions about the details of the case. That will show that you seek to understand a situation before making decisions rather than jumping straight to a solution without understanding the context. Thinking about your approach will also buy you time.
- Consider telling the interviewer what your criteria will be for your recommendation. That will show that you know how to make decisions based on clear, compelling criteria.
- Offer multiple options for consideration to show that you can generate several creative solutions. Then, recommend the option that best addresses the criteria that you selected.

Don't:
- Don't start with your recommendation. If you jump straight to the answer, you could be perceived as impulsive or lacking discernment. You want to show the employer that you can logically formulate a thoughtful answer.
- Don't act like your answer is the only correct one. I've interviewed candidates who come off as arrogant or rigid because they considered any other answer to be wrong.

For reference, here is an example of how <u>not</u> to answer a Case question like "persuade me to buy this pen from you" for someone applying for a **salesperson** role. Responsibilities for that job might include greeting customers, processing sales transactions, and answering customer questions.

"You look like the kind of person who appreciates a bargain. I'm going to explain why this pen is a good value. First, as you can see by looking at the transparent ink cartridge, it is almost completely full of ink. That means it will last a long time before running out of ink.

"Next, it's available for a low price. While pens like this often sell for $2 to $3, I'm willing to sell you this pen for the low, low price of $1.

"Finally, this pen comes with a money back guarantee. If you don't like it, I'll refund your money."

This is a disappointing answer because the candidate never bothered to understand what motivated the buyer. They jumped to the conclusion that value was the primary motivator. If the buyer was more interested in status or quality, they could be offended by the assumption that their highest priority is getting a bargain.

The candidate also didn't ask about the buyer's behavior. For example, when you formulate your sales pitch, you want to know whether the buyer currently uses pens, and if so, how. The candidate also didn't make an emotional connection with the buyer, and didn't show the customer that they cared about them in any way.

When you answer case questions, remember to ask clarifying questions and explain the criteria you are using for your answer. That way, the interviewer can see that you take a thoughtful approach to your work, and you can formulate effective recommendations based on specific circumstances related to the situation.

Now, take a few minutes to go back to the **Workbook Section** of this book, and start taking notes on your ideas for these questions.

Odd-Ball Questions

34. What Kind of Animal?

One of the strangest questions I've heard is, "If you were an animal, what would you be?" If you get a question like this, resist the urge to pick an animal that you love. Instead, pick an animal with characteristics that are relevant for the job you want.

For a city planner, a squirrel might be a good choice because they're good at preparing for the future. For a comedian, a monkey could work because they're funny and entertaining. For a security guard, consider a German Shepard because they're protective and loyal.

Don't pick an animal that's perceived negatively. You might appreciate attributes of spiders, snakes, or bats, but many people consider them scary. Don't pick a turtle because it's associated with being slow. A cat may seem like a good choice if you like cats, but they might be seen as lazy or indifferent.

Here's an amazing answer for a job as a **consultant**. Responsibilities for that role might include gathering information about an organization, analyzing business situations, and recommending new strategies to improve performance.

"I would be a hawk. I like to look at things from a high level to get a view of the big picture. Then, when I see an opportunity, I like to swoop in and get a closer look. This helps me be a good consultant because I can take a broad view of situations for my clients. Then, I can look closer to investigate specific options."

This is a great answer because the candidate connects their preferred animal to characteristics that are important in their career field. The ability to see the big picture is important for consultants, as is the ability to look closely when opportunities are identified.

Think about characteristics that an employer will value in your desired career field. Then, think of an animal that is known for those characteristics.

In an interview, you might hear variations of this question, so be prepared to answer for each of the following:

Animal: _____
Plant: _____
Type of car: _____
Famous person: _____
Piece of furniture: _____
Type of food: _____
Type of beverage: _____

Again, answer based on the characteristics that are most important in the job you want, and then explain how your selection demonstrates those characteristics.

35. Historical Person

Another odd-ball question is, "If you could have dinner with anyone from history, who would you choose?" This is a perfect opportunity to show you're always looking to expand your knowledge in your career field. Pick someone who has unique insight into your industry, and then explain how your dinner with that person would make you better at you job.

Here's a great answer for someone applying for an **electrical engineer** position. Responsibilities for that job might include designing electrical systems, evaluating electrical components, and recommending design improvements.

"I would choose Thomas Edison. His ideas for electrical engineering were ahead of their time, and I'd want to learn from his approach.

"I'd ask him how he designed his experiments and how he developed new electronic products. I'd also ask him how he organized his Invention Factory, which has fascinated me since I was a kid. I read a book about his Invention Factory when I was ten years old, and that book is a main reason I chose to pursue electrical engineering.

"I'm fascinated by the process of designing electrical systems and electronic products, and Thomas Edison was the master at that. I'd want to learn about his process for evaluating electrical components, identifying design recommendations, and building commercially-viable products."

This answer shows that the candidate has a strong passion for their career field. It also shows that the candidate is eager to learn from knowledgeable people and improve the skills needed to the do job.

In this answer, the candidate included specific examples from the job description, which I recommend you do in your answers. It demonstrates that you understand the responsibilities of the position, and you're interested in building your skills in those areas.

36. Your Most Embarrassing Moment

It might be fun in high school to ask someone, "What was your most embarrassing moment?" In an interview, this question might catch you off guard. If an interviewer asks you a question like this, resist the urge to tell an interesting story that is completely unrelated to your career.

Instead, use this question as an opportunity to tell about an important lesson that you learned. We've all had situations when we've been unprepared or we've been asked to do something embarrassing. Tell a story about one of these situations and explain what you learned from it.

Here's an example of a good answer that uses the STAR format for a **police officer** position. Responsibilities for this job could include enforcing laws, responding to emergency calls, gathering evidence, and testifying in court.

SITUATION: "Before I was a police officer, I was a security guard at a shopping mall."

TASK: "My assignment was to patrol the mall after hours to ensure that all customers were out of the building when we locked up for the night."

ACTION: "One night, I saw an elderly man trying to get into the mall by banging on a door. He wore shabby clothes, and he looked filthy. I jumped to the conclusion that he didn't belong in the mall, so I told him to go away. I threatened to notify the police and have him arrested for attempted trespassing. When I took a closer look, I realized that it was the man who owned the mall, and I was horrified that I threatened to have him arrested."

RESULT: "Through that experience, I learned to get the facts before jumping to a conclusion. The man clearly wasn't a threat to me or anyone else, so I didn't need to be alarmed. I should have calmly asked who he was and what business he had in the mall. I've learned from that experience that I should treat people with respect, get their perspective, and then assess the situation. That moment of embarrassment taught me a valuable lesson that makes me a better police officer."

I like this answer because it shows how this candidate's experience has made him better at doing the job that they're interviewing for.

Think of a few stories from your past that have taught you valuable life lessons. Practice telling those stories in ways that show how good you will be at your job. When a story is told right, it can show that even an embarrassing moment can provide experience that will make you better at your job.

37. You as a Child

If an interviewer asks you "What were you like as a child?" tell them a story that illustrates how you were born to do the type of job that they're interviewing you for.

Here's a good answer for someone applying to be a **janitor.** Responsibilities for this job might include gathering and emptying trash, cleaning restrooms, and ordering cleaning supplies.

PASSION: "I've always enjoyed organizing things, even when I was young."

EXPERIENCE: "My mom has told me stories about me as a toddler picking up my toys and putting them away every night before I went to bed. She said I would walk through a room and pick up anything that was lying on the floor.

"In elementary school, I would run around after recess to make sure all the toys were gathered and returned to the equipment room. In high school, I was the equipment manager for our athletic department because I enjoyed straightening things at the end of the day. I also enjoyed making minor repairs to the sports equipment when needed."

NEXT: "Since I like straightening things and keeping things clean, I want a job where I can do that. That's why being a janitor is a great fit for me. Some people think it's not a glamorous job, but it gives me satisfaction to know that people will come into a clean office each day because of the work I do."

This answer shows tremendous pride in doing a job well. As an interviewer, I love hearing candidates talk about the satisfaction they get from doing tasks that need to get done.

38. Your Favorite Book or Movie

Sometimes I like to ask, "What's your favorite book or movie?" to see if a candidate can connect a personal interest to the job they want. Many times, a candidate will talk about a movie that they like because it is funny or it made them cry. They completely miss the opportunity to sell the interviewer on a passion or a perspective they have that will make them a great employee.

Here's an example of an amazing answer that uses the P-E-N framework to answer this question for someone applying for a position as an **attorney.** Responsibilities for this job might include representing clients on legal matters, communicating with clients and judges, preparing legal arguments, and presenting evidence in writing and orally.

PASSION: "I've always been fascinated by books and movies that show how people can be persuaded to change their minds. For that reason, my favorite movie is an old one called *Twelve Angry Men.*"

EXPERIENCE: "Henry Fonda plays a juror in a murder trial. The other jury members think the defendant is guilty, but Henry Fonda's character thinks the defendant is *not* guilty. One by one, he persuades each juror to change their vote to not guilty. He uses a different persuasive approach for each juror based on what motivated them. For one, his argument is very logical. For another, it's emotional. The movie is like a master class on customizing your argument to your audience."

NEXT: "Since seeing that movie when I was a kid, I've wanted to have a career which requires using persuasion. That's why I want to work for your firm and become one of your most persuasive attorneys. I believe I can use my passion and experience for persuasion to benefit clients who need an advocate who is committed to their cause."

When you get a question about your favorite anything, think about what inspired you to choose your line of work. Then, tell the interviewer how that favorite anything relates to your being an effective employee in the role that they're filling.

39. Who Inspires You?

To get to know a candidate, an interviewer may ask, "Who inspires you?" This is a great question, because it reveals much about your character and values.

We all admire certain people. If a candidate says they admire someone because of their power or status, that can be a turn-off for an employer. On the other hand, if a candidate can respond with an answer that features someone with the same values as the interviewer's organization, it can demonstrate an outstanding fit for the candidate and the job.

Here's an amazing response for someone applying for a position as a **nurse**. Responsibilities for that job might include evaluating patients, administering medicines and treatments, consulting with other health professionals, and teaching patients to manage illnesses.

"I've always admired my mother. She was a nurse, and she was incredibly compassionate. She had a sense of pride in her ability to ease people's suffering.

"When I was growing up, she would tell me stories about how she helped people in her job. One time, she told me about a woman who was in the hospital for over a month. That woman had no family, and she never had visitors. My mother would go to work a few minutes early every day that month, and she'd stay a few minutes after her shift so she could spend a little time every day keeping that woman company.

"I remember hoping I would have that kind of compassion when I grew up. That's why I pursued nursing. I am passionate about caring for people. It gives me a tremendous sense of purpose to help people heal and to comfort people when they need it. That's why I'm here. I admire this hospital and your reputation for providing world-class medical care in a compassionate environment. I want to be part of that."

When you think about who inspires you, think of someone who has been a role model or a positive influence on your career. It might be a parent, a teacher, a coach, or a friend. Interviewers appreciate a personal story about someone who helped foster passion for your career path.

Avoid talking about a celebrity or political figure because they can be polarizing, and if they don't share the values of the company, your example may alienate the interviewer.

Personal examples are typically best because the interviewer will have no preconceived notions about the person. You can focus on the attributes that most closely align with the organization's culture and values. If you've researched the organization, you should be able to connect your answer with those attributes.

40. Your Tagline

An interviewer may want you to sum up yourself with a simple statement. One way to do that is to ask, "If you were a brand, what would your tagline be?" I love this question because it shows me if a candidate can communicate effectively and succinctly. It also tells me if the candidate's self-image aligns with the characteristics that I want from an employee.

Here's a great answer for someone applying for a **security guard** position. Responsibilities for that job might include providing security, enforcing laws on employer's property, and conducting security checks.

"The tagline that comes to mind is *I've got you covered*. If you hire me, I will see my role as making sure the people in this company feel safe and secure. They should feel that someone is looking out for them, their property, and the property of the company.

"They should be confident that someone is ready to step in at the first sign of trouble. That way, they can focus on their work.

"I like the phrase *I've got you covered* because it conveys a blanket of security. While people are under that blanket, they can go about their business without worries.

"I also like the term *I've* because it connotes personal responsibility. I take my job seriously, and I hold myself personally responsible to ensure all security concerns are addressed. That's why I've taken training classes and I've earned my Level 2 certification from the Department of Public Safety. I expect to have the skills needed to ensure that your people are covered."

I like this answer because the tagline connects directly with the responsibilities of the job. As you prepare for your interviews, think of a simple phrase that will summarize yourself as related to the specific job. Even if you aren't asked this question, defining your tagline will help clarify what you bring to an organization.

Odd-Ball Questions: Dos and Don'ts

With odd-ball questions, it's easy to get stumped. The key to answering them is to think about the skills you can bring to an employer. If you know what skills they want and how you can deliver those skills, you can more easily answer.

Do:
- Always respond with an answer that relates to the job you want. Your favorite animal should have characteristics that relate to the career path. Your favorite book should relate to the skills needed in the job you want. Your tagline should communicate what you bring to the organization.
- Explain the rationale for your answer. It's not enough to give a short response. Explain your answer and how it relates to what you bring to the organization.
- Be decisive. With odd-ball questions, it's tempting to say that you have many favorite animals, books, or taglines. Pick one and stand by it.

Don't:
- Don't try to be funny. It's okay to show your personality during an interview. However, if you try too hard to give humorous answers to odd-ball questions, the employer might think you're not serious about the role.
- Don't get stumped. An unprepared candidate can derail in

an interview when asked odd-ball questions. If you prepare, the interviewer will see that you can think on your feet, and that will place you above your competition.

For reference, here is an example of how a **consultant** should *not* answer the odd-ball question, "If you were an animal, what kind of animal would you be?"

"I'd be a lion. They're powerful and they command respect."

This answer is unappealing for many reasons. First, employers typically don't want employees to crave respect. They want employees who are willing to do whatever it takes to help the company succeed.

Next, being powerful is not a desirable attribute for a consultant. Consultants should be good at collaboration, problem solving, and communication. This candidate should have picked an animal that embodies one of these traits.

Finally, the answer is too brief to provide insight about the candidate. In addition to answering a question, the candidate should have included a brief explanation that connected the animal to the characteristics needed for a consultant.

These odd-ball questions give you a great opportunity to tell a quick story about your skills and make a connection between you and your desired job. Of course, that story should be brief, but it should bring to life how you're a great candidate for the open position.

Now, take a few minutes to go back to the **Workbook Section** of this book, and start taking notes on your ideas for these questions.

Closing Questions

41. Anything Else

Sometimes, interviewers will conclude their questions with, "Is there anything else I should know about you?" If they're still undecided about you, this is their way of seeing if you can make a compelling case that will sway things in your favor.

It's important that you focus on something positive for questions like this. Don't tell them that you have travel restrictions, you prefer to work certain hours, or you want a company expense account. Instead, use this question as your opportunity to tell the best story that you've prepared or to address unresolved issues from previous questions.

Here's a good example of a great answer for someone applying for a position as a **cook**. Responsibilities for this job might include checking the freshness of food ingredients and preparing food based on customer orders.

SITUATION: "I did want to mention a cooking competition that I won last year. My previous boss entered me in the Midvale Township Chili Cook-off."

TASK: "My job was to represent the restaurant with a recipe that I created for our menu."

ACTIONS: "For the competition, I went to our specialty produce supplier early that morning to get the best ingredients before other shoppers arrived. I like to do that for the restaurant, just to make sure we always have the best quality ingredients.

"Next, I made sure I had my best cooking assistant and our friendliest waitress at the competition. That way, we could always be cooking and providing the best service to the people who tried our chili.

"Finally, I picked festive bowls, napkins, and spoons for

serving the chili. Presentation is a very important part of an eating experience, so I wanted to bring great food presentation to the competition."

RESULT: "As a result, our chili beat out recipes from twenty restaurants to be selected for the grand prize. The publicity we received brought new customers into the restaurant, and sales of our chili tripled over the next few months."

With this answer, the candidate tells their best story that they hadn't yet told in the interview. As you prepare, you will likely have three or four stories that are perfect for highlighting your skills. When an interviewer asks if there's anything else you want to tell them, it's your chance to tell your best amazing story that you haven't already told during the interview.

42. References

Some employers will ask to see your references. If you're interviewing for jobs, you should have three people who you've already asked to be references for you.

I recommend you bring a list of references to the interview. On that list, include the names of three references, their relationship to you, and their preferred form of communication. That way, the employer will know whether they should contact your references via e-mail, phone call, or written letter.

These references can be anyone who is familiar with your work. Ideally, you'll have at least one previous employer on that list. The other references could be teachers, clients, coworkers, or people from organizations where you've volunteered.

Avoid using family members and friends as references since they won't be considered impartial judges of your capabilities. You also don't need to include your current employer on your list of references. Since they may not know that you're looking for work, an interviewer will not expect you to list them as a reference.

Here's a good answer to this question about reference for someone applying for a position as a **bookkeeper.** Responsibilities for this job might include documenting financial transactions, analyzing data, and developing financial recommendations.

"Here is a list of three people who have agreed to be my references. The first is my previous employer who has since left the company where I currently work. She was my boss for over a year, so she's the best judge of my capabilities.

"Next is the volunteer coordinator for the animal shelter where I volunteer. I help them with their bookkeeping, so he can also attest to my bookkeeping skills.

"The third person on this list is my faculty advisor who worked with me when I was getting my accounting degree. She supervised me on several class projects, so she's familiar with my academic work."

I like this answer because it includes people who have a wide variety of experience with candidate. They can provide input related to work experience and academic capabilities. For your references, try to get people who have directly supervised you in a variety of experiences.

43. What Questions Do You Have?

Typically, interviews end with the employer asking you if you have any questions. This is your chance to put the interviewer in the position of selling the job to you.

Don't ask questions that pressure the interviewer to tell why you shouldn't work for the company or what they don't like about the job. This will make them think they shouldn't offer you a job.

Don't ask about salary, benefits, or work hours. You can negotiate that once you have an offer.

Do get them talking about why they like the company or why they think you would be a good fit for the role. Also, interviewers love giving advice. Don't we all? So, ask their advice for someone who might be joining their organization. That way, they'll be giving you advice as if you were their new employee. This has a powerful subliminal effect of transitioning their perspective from evaluating you to thinking of you as an incoming employee.

Here are a few great questions to ask at the end of an interview:

"What do you like most about working for this organization?"

"What characteristics are most important when you consider candidates for this role?"

"What advice would you give someone coming into this role?"

Again, these questions allow the interviewer to tell you how wonderful their organization is. You want them to go into selling mode. If they're selling you on the job or the organization, they are more likely to see you in the role they're trying to fill.

Also, if you ask the interviewer for their advice, it will show them that you value their perspective. Plus, people tend to want to help those who ask for advice. If the interview has gone well, they might be inclined to help by extending a job offer.

44. When Could You Start?

If you prepare properly, there is a chance your interview could end with your being asked "When can you start?" Even if you don't get this question during the interview, you should prepare for it, since it will hopefully come shortly after the interview.

Answer this question truthfully. (Of course, you should answer every question truthfully, but for this question, candidates sometimes respond with what they think the interviewer wants to hear rather that what's realistic.) If you're required to give your current employer two weeks' notice, tell the interviewer that.

Also, it's okay to ask when the interviewer would like to fill the role. If they are flexible on the start date, you could negotiate with them. They might be agreeable to having you delay your start date so you can take some time off between jobs. However, they might also need someone to start as soon as possible. You won't know unless you ask, so I recommend you ask.

Here's a good response to this question.

"Do you have a specific date in mind when you want someone to start in this role? I'm required to give my current employer two weeks' notice, which I could do as soon as we negotiate the details of the offer. However, if you want someone to start later, I would be open to giving notice to my current employer, then taking a short period of time off before starting work with you. Let me know what works best for you."

This is a great answer because it shows a strong interest in the job, but it also shows that the candidate expects to negotiate a fair offer. You want to seem interested, but don't give the impression that you'll accept any offer. Given the opportunity, you should signal that you'll be interested in an offer, and you expect it to be a fair one.

Closing Questions: Dos and Don'ts

With closing questions, you want to end the interview on a positive note. Here are a few tips for doing that:

Do:
- Put the employer in the mode of selling the job to you. The best way to do this is to ask them what you would like most about working for them.
- Be prepared with a list of references. On that list, include your relationship with your references and their preferred form of communication.
- If you have the opportunity, tell the employer the top reason they should hire you, or give them the best example of your most relevant accomplishment.
- If you want the job, tell the interviewer that. They want to offer the position to someone who really wants it, so tell them you want it.

Don't:

- Don't ask the interviewer to tell you anything negative about the company. You don't want them to tell you why you shouldn't work there.
- Don't ask about salary, benefits, or work hours. You can negotiate those details once you have an offer. If you ask about these during an interview, the employer will think you're only motivated by compensation or easy working hours. You want them to know that you're motivated because you love the type of work they offer and you'll be a great fit for their company.

For reference, here is an example of how *not* to answer a closing question like, "What questions do you have?"

"First, what are the aspects of the company that you like least?"

"Second, how many weeks of vacation will I get if I decide to work here?"

"Third, how fast can I get promoted?"

I've actually had candidates ask all three of these questions at the end of interviews. If the candidates were in the running before they asked these questions, I quickly ruled them out.

Remember, the point of the interview is for you to sell the interviewer on why you're a great fit for their open role. You should close the interview by leaving the impression that you have fantastic skills, you're highly motivated, and you'll be a great addition to their team.

Don't end the interview by leaving a final impression that you're looking for reasons to dislike the company, you just care about benefits, or you want to get promoted faster than what might be realistic.

Now, take a few minutes to go back to the **Workbook Section** of this book, and start taking notes on your ideas for these questions.

Conclusion

Thank you for reading this book. I hope you've enjoyed it, and I hope it helps you build the interview skills you need to get your dream job.

Here are a few final tips for becoming an amazing interviewer.

Customize your answers:

Remember, getting the job description is like getting the answers to a test ahead of time. In the job description, the employer tells you exactly what they want to hear during the interview. You just need to customize your answers to match the job description.

You should highlight your experiences that are most relevant for that specific job. The employer isn't interested in your experiences that are unrelated to the position they are trying to fill. Those experiences might be important to you, but they're not important to the employer. Spend every minute of your precious interview time talking about experiences and skills that the employer will value in the role they have to fill.

Practice, practice, practice:

The next section of this book is designed to help you practice. It includes the same 44 questions that you've read in this book, but I've included 44 different amazing answers. That way, you'll have two examples of great answers for each question.

I've also included pages with space for you to write your answer to each question. Please use those pages as a workbook where you take notes, make corrections, and refine your answers. Feel free to copy the blank pages so you have worksheets to use as you update your answers.

Find interview partners or coaches:

It helps to have someone who will provide feedback on your interview answers. If possible, find someone in the same type of job that you want, and ask them to practice with you.

If you're a student or if you know people in your career field who may be job hunting in the near future, you could form an interview group with them.

When I was in business school, we formed a group of four people who met twice a week to practice interviewing. We would ask each other questions and give each other advice on our answers. It was the most productive team that I've ever been a part of.

If you have classmates, friends, co-workers, or family members who are willing to be your interview team members, coaches, or sounding boards, please take advantage of that. Find people who want you to succeed, and commit to meeting with them on a regular basis. I recommend practicing at least two hours a week, or more if your schedule allows.

If you're in school, see if your school has a career development office. People there may be willing to coach you for free. You might want to give them a copy of this book so they can see how you're approaching your questions. Then, schedule practice sessions with them to have them assess your interview answers.

Also, your community may have job service centers or workforce centers that offer interview training. You might want to call them to see if they have interview coaches or if they can help you build an interview team.

I don't recommend that you pay for professional

interview coaches unless you are seeking a highly-competitive job in a high-paying field. Professional coaches can help, but you should have all the tools you need in this book. Hopefully, you can find someone who will practice with you for no charge.

There are many other lessons in this book, so I hope you find content that is useful.

I have one request. Please take a minute to rate this book and write a review in the online store where you purchased it. Thanks again, and best wishes as you develop your own amazing interview answers.

Workbook Section

I've included this section as a workbook where you can write your customized answers for interview questions. To inspire you, I've included one more amazing answer for each question. Next to those answers, you'll find blank templates where you can write your own amazing answers based on your specific passions, experiences, and goals.

I recommend you write in pencil, or if you prefer, type your answers using a computer. That way, you can make revisions and improvements as you practice.

Remember to practice your answers with friends, classmates, family members, career counselors, or anyone else who will listen to you. They can give you tips for improving your responses until each one is amazing.

Before you begin, remember to write a summary job description for the position you want. Refer to this job description as you craft your answers so you stay focused on responses that will appeal to your interviewer. To see examples of summary job descriptions, go to the section titled **Sample Job Descriptions** starting on page 211.

Job Title: _English Teacher_

Responsibilities: _- classroom environment conducive to learning_
- guides learning process toward achievement of curriculum goals
- use a variety of instructional techniques and instructional technology

1. Tell Me about Yourself

Question: "Tell me about yourself."

Job Title:	**Construction Worker**
Responsibilities:	Follow construction plans and supervisor instructions to build structures, load and unload building materials, and operate tools needed during construction process

PASSION: "I've always loved building things."

EXPERIENCE: "When I was kid, I spent hours making structures with building blocks, testing them, and finding ways to make them stronger. My favorite class in high school was shop class. I was always the first person to class, and I would stay after school to work on projects. I worked with the teacher to learn the best ways to use every available tool, from the simplest hand tools to the most complex power tools.

"Since graduating from high school last year, I've been working for a small builder in the area on construction sites for single family homes. It's great work, but the builder is going out of business."

NEXT: "Now, I'm looking for a construction job with a builder who has an established business and a reputation for building high-quality homes. I take pride in my work, and I want to work where quality is valued."

Write your answer to this question here:

PASSION: I've always wanted to be a teacher to make a difference in students' lives.

EXPERIENCE: It's all because, year after year, my teachers made a huge impression me, and I wanted to be that for others. For the past three years, I've been selected by Top Scholars as their "Most Influential Teacher." This is truly a cherished honor for ~~be~~ me because all that I do is for my students' success in the classroom, but more importantly, to show them their worth, potential,

NEXT: and ability to form their own opinions by thinking critically and observing the world around them.

I'm looking for a teaching position in a school community I can truly call "home" and have the greatest impact in.

★ memo.
they
cared
about me

121

2. Walk Me through Your Resume

Question: "Walk me through your resume."

Job Title:	**Detective**
Responsibilities:	Analyze crime scenes, collect evidence, interview witnesses and suspects, and solve crimes

PASSION: "I've always had a strong sense of justice and a passion for getting to the truth."

EXPERIENCE: "As you can see on my resume, I led the cadet ethics board while I was at the police academy. While there, I investigated, built cases, and determined judgments for ethics violations.

"In my first job as a police officer, I was a beat cop in a very tough part of town. In that role, I investigated crimes, collected evidence, and interviewed witnesses. While there, I helped solve three high-profile cases, which I can tell you more about if you like.

"As a beat cop, I worked closely with the detectives in our department, and their work appealed to me."

NEXT: "Now, I'm looking for a role where I have more responsibility for investigating crimes. While I like being a beat cop, my true passion is the type of work that detectives do."

Write your answer to this question here:

PASSION: I'm passionate about being a lifelong learner.

EXPERIENCE: As you can see on my resume, I've taught all grade levels and course levels. I've jumped at every opportunity to teach different classes to better hone my craft and grow in my content knowledge. Most recently, I completed my Masters in English and started an on-campus dual enrollment program through Cincinnati State.

*from 9th grade CP english to ENG 103 and AP English

NEXT: Now, I'm looking to continue preparing students for similar advanced or dual credit so that they are better set up for success after graduation.

* save money on total college cost

3. Why Should I Hire You?

Question: "Why should I hire you?"

Job Title: **Graphic Designer**

Responsibilities: Work with design software, create compelling visual concepts, develop impactful layouts, and prepare graphic files for production

PASSION: "I've always loved finding new ways to bring ideas to life."

EXPERIENCE: "When I was in high school, I led the design staff for our school newspaper, and I redesigned the newspaper layout that our school had been using for decades. I also designed a new digital newsletter that students could use to post photos and comments themselves.

"In my current job, I'm leading the redesign of the marketing materials for the agency's top three clients. I'm also in charge of finding new design software programs and training our team members to use those programs as we implement them.

"My school newspaper designs and examples of work from my current job are in my portfolio, which I've brought for you to review if you like."

NEXT: "If you hire me, I'll bring that passion for finding new ways to bring ideas to life in your agency for your clients."

Write your answer to this question here:

PASSION: I'm a dedicated, organized, and compassionate teacher who wants to reach as many lives as possible.

EXPERIENCE: I carefully plan my lessons and units with my students in mind. I create activities and assignments with various educational technology tools. I'm fluent in all things Google and get so much satisfaction out of creating eye-catching graphic organizers that help students chunk information and NEXT: tasks to assist them with an end result, while selecting texts that are engaging and relateable.

4. Why Are You a Good Candidate?

Question: "Why are you a good candidate for this job?"

Job Title:	**Office Clerk**
Responsibilities:	Answer phone calls, take messages, schedule appointments, greet visitors, and prepare letters and other office documents

PASSION: "I understand you want to build an office team that provides top quality customer service. I've always had a passion for customer service, and I can be a strong addition to your team."

EXPERIENCE: "In my current job as a receptionist, I enjoy answering phone calls, taking messages, and scheduling appointments. I've consistently received high marks on my evaluations, especially in customer service and teamwork.

"I have extensive experience with word processing and spreadsheet programs. In high school, I worked on our school's newspaper as a copy editor and budget coordinator."

NEXT: "I'm looking for a role where I can use my passion for customer service as part of a high-quality office team. I also want to use my word processing and spreadsheet skills to prepare letters and other documents that deliver impactful communications for our team and our customers. I think I'd be a great candidate for this job."

Write your answer to this question here:

PASSION: _____

_____

_____

EXPERIENCE: _____

_____

_____

_____

_____

_____

_____

_____

_____

_____

NEXT: _____

_____

_____

_____

_____

_____

5. Why Did You Leave Your Last Job?

Question: "Why did you leave your last job?"

Job Title:	**Paralegal**
Responsibilities:	Research laws and regulations, write reports to help attorneys prepare for trials, and file briefs with the court

PASSION: "I'm passionate about becoming a skilled researcher and having a meaningful impact in my job. I left my last job because I returned to school to get my associate's degree in paralegal studies. That degree will help me pursue those passions in my career."

EXPERIENCE: "In the small legal firm where I previously worked, I was an office clerk. I'm not applying to go back there because the firm doesn't have the opportunities I want to advance my skills as a paralegal.

"That firm handles primarily simple traffic cases, and there is little research involved in those cases. My role was to answer phones, schedule meetings, and file briefs. It was great experience, but it's not what I want to do long term."

NEXT: "Now, I'm looking for a role where I can do the type of work that I'm passionate about, which includes researching laws and writing reports to help attorneys prepare for trials. I'm still interested in filing briefs, which is something I enjoy. I want to do more, and hopefully I'll have that opportunity here."

Write your answer to this question here:

PASSION: _____

_____

_____

EXPERIENCE: _____

_____

_____

_____

_____

_____

_____

_____

_____

_____

_____

NEXT: _____

_____

_____

_____

_____

_____

6. Your Favorite Job

Question: "Of all your jobs, which was your favorite?"

Job Title:	**Pharmaceutical Sales Rep**
Responsibilities:	Build relationships with healthcare providers, sell portfolio of pharmaceutical products, resolve customer inquiries and complaints, and document all customer interactions

PASSION: "I've always loved people. I enjoy getting to know them, hearing about their lives, and helping them accomplish their goals."

EXPERIENCE: "My favorite job was when I worked as a sales assistant for a home builder. In that role, I got to know our customers and what they wanted in their homes.

"My job was to build relationships with them and to maintain those relationships throughout the building process, which typically lasted a few months. I would address their issues and document our interactions. It was my favorite job because it allowed me to build relationships with customers and help them accomplish their goals."

NEXT: "Now, I'm looking for a role where I can build longer and stronger relationships. I have a passion for healthcare and a bachelor's degree in biology, so I'm looking for a sales job in the medical field. I think your role might be a perfect fit since it would allow me to build relationships and help healthcare providers accomplish their goals of providing quality care for their patients."

Write your answer to this question here:

PASSION: _____

_____

_____

EXPERIENCE: _____

_____

_____

_____

_____

_____

_____

_____

_____

_____

NEXT: _____

_____

_____

_____

_____

_____

7. Your Least Favorite Job

Question: "Of your jobs, which was your least favorite?"

Job Title: **Reporter**

Responsibilities: Research topics, interview people, write articles, edit, and submit articles prior to publication deadlines

PASSION: "I've always loved journalism because I never know where a story will take me, and I enjoy that process of discovery as I uncover the story."

EXPERIENCE: "My least favorite job was when I worked as a waitress in college. It was in a fast-paced restaurant, and every day was the same. While customers would order different things off the menu and have different questions, there was never an opportunity to uncover the what, who, where, when, and why of their stories.

"I enjoyed the pace of the job. I like it when things move quickly because that's the way I'm wired. But I didn't like the repetitive nature of serving the customers and experiencing the same process over and over."

NEXT: "I'm looking for a role with a similar fast pace, but with more variety in the work. I want to dig into different topics and see where the stories lead me. I want to discover the details and share them with readers, which is why I believe this role will be a great fit for me."

Write your answer to this question here:

PASSION: _____

_____

_____

EXPERIENCE: _____

_____

_____

_____

_____

_____

_____

_____

_____

_____

NEXT: _____

_____

_____

_____

_____

8. What Would You Do First?

Question: "If I hired you, what would you do first?"

Job Title:	**Personal Care Aide**
Responsibilities:	Assist clients with daily tasks, engage clients with physical and mental activity, and perform basic housekeeping tasks

"I'm glad you asked. I took the liberty of creating a 30-60-90 Day Plan to show you how I might approach this job."

30 DAYS: "In the first 30 days, I'd like to master the tasks required for helping my client. I'd also like to build a rapport with them by getting to know what's important to them. If they have family members, I'd like to meet them and see what role they'd like to play in the client's care."

60 DAYS: "In the next 30 days, I'd like to see what services I could provide beyond the basics of helping them with daily tasks. Maybe I could help them pursue an interest or develop a hobby. I believe personal care involves both mental and physical aspects."

90 DAYS: "In the 30 days after that, I'd like to see what else I could do to make life better for my client and their loved ones. Maybe it would involve helping them find a social group if they're up for it, or getting them to spend more time outdoors."

"Those are a few ideas. Do you have other suggestions?"

Write your answer to this question here:

30 DAYS: _____

_____

_____

_____

_____

_____

60 DAYS: _____

_____

_____

_____

_____

_____

90 DAYS: _____

_____

_____

_____

_____

_____

9. How Soon Could You Make an Impact?

Question: "How soon could you make an impact here?"

Job Title:	**Teaching Assistant**
Responsibilities:	Tutor students in small groups or one-on-one, supervise students when teacher is unavailable, enforce classroom rules, and help teacher prepare lessons and grade papers

"I plan to have an immediate impact. Here are a few ideas that come to mind."

30 DAYS: "In my first 30 days, I would like to schedule regular meetings with the teachers I'm assisting to see where they need help. I'd want to clarify their expectations and define specific tasks for myself. Then, I would immediately start doing those tasks, which could include grading papers, tutoring students, and supervising the classroom when a teacher isn't available."

60 DAYS: "In the next 30 days, I'd like to get an understanding of individual student's needs. For example, when I grade papers, I could see which students might benefit from extra tutoring."

90 DAYS: "In the 30 days after that, I'd like to offer suggestions to teachers for improving their lesson plans or classroom processes. I know teachers are the leaders in the classroom, but if they're open to suggestions, I'd like to offer ideas."

Write your answer to this question here:

30 DAYS: _____

_____

_____

_____

_____

_____

60 DAYS: _____

_____

_____

_____

_____

_____

90 DAYS: _____

_____

_____

_____

_____

_____

10. Why Are You Interested in this Job?

Question: "Why are you interested in this job?"

Job Title: **Painter**
Responsibilities: Prepare rooms by covering surfaces, prepare surfaces by sanding and scraping loose paint, apply primers and paint, and clean rooms after painting procedures are done

PASSION: "I've always loved working with my hands, and I've enjoyed painting since I was a kid."

EXPERIENCE: "My dad used to be a handyman, and I would go with him on jobs. My favorite part was helping him prepare rooms for painting and cleaning up afterwards. I also enjoyed the painting process.

"While I was in high school, I would make money on the weekends by helping people with painting jobs. My customers would regularly hire me to come back and paint additional rooms when they needed a painter, which gave me a tremendous sense of satisfaction."

NEXT: "Now that I'm graduating from high school, I'm looking for a job where I can paint full time. I know everything that's involved with prepping, painting, and cleaning up. I enjoy that kind of work. I'm also good with customers, and I love seeing that they're satisfied with a job well done. That's why I want this job."

Write your answer to this question here:

PASSION: _____

_____

_____

EXPERIENCE: _____

_____

_____

_____

_____

_____

_____

_____

_____

NEXT: _____

_____

_____

_____

_____

_____

11. What Are Your Goals?

Question: "What are your goals?"

Job Title:	**Computer Technician**
Responsibilities:	Install and repair computer hardware, install and update software, troubleshoot computer issues, and provide technical support to company personnel

PASSION: "My goal is to become a master technician for computer hardware systems and software installations."

EXPERIENCE: "As you can see from my resume, I have a computer science degree from a technical school, and I'm proficient with a wide variety of computer platforms. I have also been building computer networks since I was a kid.

"In high school, I rebuilt the entire network for our school's computer lab. I reconfigured the existing hardware and changed the internet provider to create a network that ran 80% faster with no increase in cost.

"I've also been working on the computer network at the church I attend. I'm responsible for installing and maintaining new software programs."

NEXT: "Now, my immediate goal is to get a job as a computer technician at your company, because you have the highest standards in information technology. I'd like to work here and build my skills so I can reach my goal of becoming a master technician and having a career doing what I enjoy most."

Write your answer to this question here:

PASSION: _____

_____

_____

EXPERIENCE: _____

_____

_____

_____

_____

_____

_____

_____

_____

_____

NEXT: _____

_____

_____

_____

_____

_____

12. What Would You Want from this Job?

Question: "What would you want from this job?"

Job Title:	**Childcare Worker**
Responsibilities:	Supervise and maintain safety of children, organize activities to entertain and educate children, serve food and change diapers as needed, and keep records of progress and issues with children

PASSION: "I've always loved taking care of children. In my next job, I want the satisfaction of providing excellent childcare, which to me means organizing activities that entertain and educate. It also means taking care of the daily needs of babies and toddlers such as feeding and changing diapers."

EXPERIENCE: "Since I was a kid, I was always looking after my younger siblings. In high school, I was a babysitter for three years, even completing my babysitting certificate with the Red Cross."

NEXT: "Now, I'd like to get a full-time job where I can take care of kids. My preference is to work with younger kids, from newborns to preschool age. Most of my babysitting was done with kids that age, and that's what I enjoy most."

Write your answer to this question here:

PASSION: _____

_____

_____

EXPERIENCE: _____

_____

_____

_____

_____

_____

_____

_____

_____

NEXT: _____

_____

_____

_____

_____

_____

13. Make Yourself More Effective

Question: "What do you do to be more effective at your job?"

Job Title:	**Welder**
Responsibilities:	Read blueprints and design specifications, weld metal parts together, and maintain equipment

PASSION: "I love finding new ways to improve my skills."

EXPERIENCE: "In high school, I would stay late to practice my welding skills in my school's shop. After graduation, I took a welding class at a technical college, and I've completed the work needed to become a certified welder with the American Welding Society.

"In my garage, I have a welding torch, and I've been working on metal sculptures. I've even entered a few of my sculptures in contests. Last year, one of my sculptures won second place in the Centerville Art Festival sculpture contest.

"I also read the publications including the *Welding Journal* and *Practical Welding Today* to stay on top of the latest welding techniques and technology."

NEXT: "In my next job, I hope to continue building my welding skills and become even more effective at my trade."

Write your answer to this question here:

PASSION: _____

_____

_____

EXPERIENCE: _____

_____

_____

_____

_____

_____

_____

_____

_____

_____

NEXT: _____

_____

_____

_____

_____

_____

14. How Did You Hear about Us?

Question: "How did you hear about us?"

Job Title:	**Store Clerk**
Responsibilities:	Greet customers and answer questions they might have, recommend merchandise to meet customer needs, process payment transactions, and restock items as needed

PASSION: "I've been a customer at your store for years. I love shopping here, and I love the brands you carry."

EXPERIENCE: "I first heard about your store from a friend who suggested I shop here. She told me about your great service and selection. I've been impressed every time I came here. I remember one time there was a jacket that I liked, but it wasn't available in my size. The salesperson contacted another store and had them send it to this store the next day. The salesperson called me when it arrived and let me know that it had been set aside for me. When I arrived to pick it up, that salesperson even helped me choose a scarf that looked great with the jacket."

NEXT: "I want to work where that level of customer service is encouraged. I've always gone the extra mile to provide outstanding service, and I'd like to do that while working here."

Write your answer to this question here:

PASSION: _____

_____

_____

EXPERIENCE: _____

_____

_____

_____

_____

_____

_____

_____

_____

NEXT: _____

_____

_____

_____

_____

_____

15. Demonstrate Leadership

Question: "Tell me about a time you demonstrated leadership?"

Question Variations: "Tell me about a time you demonstrated persuasion, teamwork, results, or other similar skills."

Job Title: **Production Manager**
Responsibilities: Supervise production workers, ensure production goals are met, and ensure the safety of all workers

SITUATION: "I was a shift worker at Apex Fabricators."

TASK: "My job was to work on the assembly line adding bearings to car axels as they came down the line."

ACTION: "I noticed the production line would back up because of a slowdown at the station before me, so I asked my shift manager if I could troubleshoot the issue. She agreed, so I formed a small team that included our plant maintenance specialist and our operations manager. I explained the issue to them, and I asked for their input. We watched the production process together, and I noticed the workers in that station had to walk back and forth to get parts they needed. I worked with the maintenance expert to reconfigure that station to put the parts inventory closer to the assembly line."

RESULTS: "As a result, the workers at that station were able to reduce their assembly time by 5 seconds, which improved the throughput for the entire line by 3%."

Write your answer to this question here:

SITUATION: _____

_____

_____

TASK: _____

_____

_____

ACTION: _____

_____

_____

_____

_____

_____

_____

RESULT: _____

_____

_____

_____

16. Demonstrate Creativity

Question: "Tell me about a time you demonstrated creativity?"
Question Variations: "Tell me about a time you demonstrated out-of-the-box thinking or developed an innovative solution to a challenging problem."

Job Title:	**Cafeteria Worker**
Responsibilities:	Prepare and cook food, greet and serve customers, and clean work areas and cooking equipment

SITUATION: "My example happened when I was working in a cafeteria at Middleton Elementary School."

TASK: "My job was to prepare food for lunches that would be served the next day."

ACTION: "While I was prepping one day, I noticed we were almost out of cheese. Our featured item the next day was macaroni and cheese, so being low on cheese was an issue. I immediately started looking for substitutes. I'm a big cheese puff fan, so I wondered if we could substitute cheese puffs for cheese. I worked with the cook, and after experimenting, we came up with a recipe I called *Crispy Puffy Mac N Cheese*."

RESULTS: "The result was a delicious dish that was a big hit with the kids. We now serve that recipe every Wednesday, and it's our top seller. Several schools in our district are also serving the recipe now, and it's become their top seller as well. And to think, it all happened because we were running low on cheese."

Write your answer to this question here:

SITUATION: _____

_____

_____

TASK: _____

_____

_____

ACTION: _____

_____

_____

_____

_____

_____

_____

RESULT: _____

_____

_____

_____

17. Demonstrate Collaboration

Question: "Tell me about a time you demonstrated collaboration?"

Question Variations: "Tell me about a time you demonstrated interpersonal skills or an ability to work with others."

Job Title:	**Physician**
Responsibilities:	Diagnose and treat medical issues, order and interpret medical tests, and develop treatment plans

SITUATION: "I was working as a medical resident."

TASK: "My job was to order medical tests and to interpret them for patients at Hilltop Hospital."

ACTION: "One time, I ordered medical tests for a patient who was showing symptoms of food allergies. The results came back negative. The patient's condition got progressively worse, so I assembled a team of specialists to discuss the case. I reviewed the case with them, gave them an overview of the symptoms and test results, and asked for their input. After extensive discussion and follow-up tests, I determined the patient had a rare virus which caused the symptoms."

RESULTS: "As a result, we were able to save the patient. I believe my ability to assemble a team of problem solving experts can be used to deliver top quality treatment for patients like that individual."

Write your answer to this question here:

SITUATION: _____

_____

_____

TASK: _____

_____

_____

ACTION: _____

_____

_____

_____

_____

_____

_____

RESULT: _____

_____

_____

_____

18. Demonstrate Analytical Skills

Question: "Tell me about a time you demonstrated analytical skills?"

Question variations: "Tell me about a time you demonstrated an ability to solve complex problems or think strategically."

Job Title:	**Mechanical Engineer**
Responsibilities:	Design mechanical systems and devices, develop prototypes, and oversee manufacturing processes

SITUATION: "I was working as an intern at a small engineering firm."

TASK: "My job was to help develop prototypes for a new line of portable electrical generators."

ACTION: "We were having issues with our prototypes because they would get so hot that they would stop working. I researched a variety of materials that we could use. Then, I analyzed data related to heat resistance, cooling properties, and durability to find options. My analysis showed that a new synthetic polymer would be a good option, so I started making prototypes using that polymer."

RESULTS: "As a result, I was able to build prototypes that had the right heat resistance and cooling properties for our generators. The engineering firm still uses that polymer for most of the prototypes they build to this day."

Write your answer to this question here:

SITUATION: _____

_____

_____

TASK: _____

_____

_____

ACTION: _____

_____

_____

_____

_____

_____

_____

_____

RESULT: _____

_____

_____

_____

19. Demonstrate Flexibility

Question: "Tell me about a time you demonstrated flexibility?"

Job Title:	**Delivery Person**
Responsibilities:	Load and unload cargo, drive variety of delivery vehicles, and document deliveries

SITUATION: "I was working as a delivery person for a medical supplies company."

TASK: "One time, my supervisor gave me a top priority package and said it had to be delivered by 10 a.m."

ACTIONS: "While I was driving to the delivery address, I came to a place where the road was flooded. There was no way through, and no other roads would have gotten me to the destination on time. I noticed a footbridge that would get me over the flooded area, so I secured my truck in a nearby parking lot, grabbed the package, and went to the footbridge. I requested an Uber driver to pick me up on the other side, and I got the package to the destination on time."

RESULTS: "It turns out that the package was needed for an organ transplant that morning. I later found out that because I got the package there on time, the surgeons were able to proceed with the transplant which saved the life of a patient. Now, I treat every top priority package like it's mission critical. I will find a way to deliver it no matter how flexible I need to be."

Write your answer to this question here:

SITUATION: _____

_____

_____

TASK: _____

_____

_____

ACTION: _____

_____

_____

_____

_____

_____

_____

RESULT: _____

_____

_____

_____

20. Demonstrate Persistence

Question: "Tell me about a time you demonstrated persistence."

Question variations: "Tell me about a time you demonstrated an ability to work through a challenging situation or you accomplished something when others would have given up."

Job Title: **Computer Systems Administrator**

Responsibilities: Design computer systems, and troubleshoot computer issues

SITUATION: "I was working as a computer technician for a small software development company."

TASK: "My job was to fix issues on the servers."

ACTION: "We had one server array that kept going down. Several technicians tried to fix it before I was called in, and none of them were able to get it working. I went through the manufacturer's checklist, and nothing solved the issue. I then searched online forums, computer blogs, and video sites with no success. Finally, I found a technician in Singapore who posted a solution in the comments section of a blog site."

RESULTS: "Because of my persistence, I was able to find a solution to an issue that had stumped other technicians. That solution allowed me to fix a $100,000 server that has worked well ever since."

Write your answer to this question here:

SITUATION: _____
_____
_____

TASK: _____
_____
_____

ACTION: _____
_____
_____
_____
_____
_____
_____

RESULT: _____
_____
_____
_____

21. A Decision You Regretted

Question: "Tell me about a time you made a decision you regretted."

Job Title:	**Assembler and Fabricator**
Responsibilities:	Read assembly instructions and blueprints, use hand tools and power tools to assemble parts, and conduct quality control checks

SITUATION: "I was working as an assembler at a toy manufacturing plant."

TASK: "My assignment was to assemble the support structure for our large doll houses."

ACTION: "One day, I noticed that a batch of our parts contained defective pieces. My coworker told me to use the parts anyway because we had to meet our quota. I did as my coworker instructed. That night, I couldn't sleep. I felt like something was wrong, and I couldn't accept that I would be responsible for defective products. The next morning, I told my supervisor about the issue. He contacted the supplier, and we were able to get replacement parts and install them in the doll houses."

RESULTS: "I should have notified my supervisor as soon as I recognized the issue. As a result of this experience I've learned to immediately notify my supervisor of issues. Together, we can decide how to proceed, which will ensure we provide quality products in a timely way."

Write your answer to this question here:

SITUATION: _____

_____

_____

TASK: _____

_____

_____

ACTION: _____

_____

_____

_____

_____

_____

_____

RESULT: _____

_____

_____

_____

22. Address Competing Priorities

Question: "Tell me how you address competing priorities."

Job Title:	**Baker**
Responsibilities:	Check quality of baking ingredients, prepare dough, bake variety of breads and other baked goods, decorate food items, and maintain food safety standards

SITUATION: "In my current job, I'm the baker for a small grocery store."

TASK: "One day, I received more custom orders than we could possibly produce, including eight birthday cakes, two wedding cakes, ninety custom donuts, and fifty cupcakes."

ACTION: "I immediately started thinking about options for producing the orders. I started by seeing if I could find anyone to help. Because I have good relationships with other bakers in the area, I was able to find a colleague to produce the cupcakes. I contacted the customer who ordered the donuts, and I offered to deliver them if they could wait an extra day for the order. They happily agreed. That left me with the cakes, which we could do based on our regular workload."

RESULTS: "Because I was able to leverage my relationships with other bakers and clarify the needs of customers, we were able to handle the competing priorities and deliver all orders with 100% customer satisfaction."

Write your answer to this question here:

SITUATION: _____

_____

_____

TASK: _____

_____

_____

ACTION: _____

_____

_____

_____

_____

_____

_____

RESULT: _____

_____

_____

_____

23. Your Greatest Strength

Question: "What is your greatest strength?"

Job Title:	**Purchasing Agent**
Responsibilities:	Identify and maintain relationships with suppliers, negotiate contracts, and enforce procedures for defective or delayed supplies or services

"I'd say my greatest strength is my ability to negotiate."

SITUATION: "Let me give you an example from when I negotiated contracts for a fundraising event."

TASK: "My role was to secure a venue and catering company for the event."

ACTION: "I always start by seeing if potential suppliers have goals that we can help them with. For the venue, I found one option that was a new banquet hall just opening for business. I offered to provide free publicity for their site since our fundraiser included attendees from meeting planning companies. For the caterer, I found a restaurant chain that was expanding into the area. They told me that they also wanted publicity for their new location, which I could provide."

RESULTS: "Because I did a good job determining the goals for potential suppliers, I was able to identify businesses that needed us as much as we needed them. I was able to get the venue and catering for less than half the anticipated cost because I offered them publicity that was important to them but free for us to provide."

Write your answer to this question here:

SITUATION: _____

_____

_____

TASK: _____

_____

_____

ACTION: _____

_____

_____

_____

_____

_____

_____

_____

RESULT: _____

_____

_____

_____

24. Your Biggest Weakness

Question: "What is your biggest weakness?"

Job Title: **Truck Driver**
Responsibilities: Inspect truck and trailer before and after trips, drive long distances, comply with all traffic laws, maintain vehicle in good working order, and maintain log of driving time and any incidents

"I'd say my biggest weakness is that I'm not very outgoing."

SITUATION: "When I graduated from high school, I took a job in sales for a restaurant supply company."

TASK: "My job was to generate new customers."

ACTION: "That meant I had to go door-to-door calling on restaurant managers. I found that after a few hours, I would get really tired. I could be friendly and polite to potential customers, but it wore me out to be talking with people all day. The company had an opening for a long-haul delivery driver, which I took and I've loved it ever since."

RESULTS: "Through that experience, I've learned that I'm really an introvert. I enjoy jobs that I can do on my own. I also learned that I really enjoy driving, especially the longer delivery routes. That's why I changed my focus to become a truck driver."

Write your answer to this question here:

SITUATION: _____

_____

_____

TASK: _____

_____

_____

ACTION: _____

_____

_____

_____

_____

_____

_____

RESULT: _____

_____

_____

_____

25. Your Tolerance for Risk

Question: "What is your tolerance for risk?"

Job Title:	**Store Manager**
Responsibilities:	Supervise staff, ensure proper operations of store, and ensure sales goals are met

"I'd say I enjoy taking calculated risks."

SITUATION: "In my current job, I'm an assistant manager for a pet supply store."

TASK: "One of my tasks is to develop our marketing promotions."

ACTION: "I really enjoy trying new things, especially when I have some insight as to what might work. I like to gather input from customers and employees about new ideas. Then, I like to try those ideas and measure the results. One example is when I organized a fun run that customers could do with their dogs. It was something we'd never tried before, which made it risky. I knew some of our customers jogged with their dogs, so I thought the event might work."

RESULTS: "The result was outstanding. We had over 100 customers at the first event, and many told their friends. Over 200 people attended the second event. Since then, we started having the fun runs monthly, and the attendance has grown every month, as has our customer base."

Write your answer to this question here:

SITUATION: _____
_____
_____

TASK: _____
_____
_____

ACTION: _____
_____
_____
_____
_____
_____
_____
_____

RESULT: _____
_____
_____
_____

26. Your Friends' Description of You

Question: "How would your friends describe you?"

Job Title: **Quality Control Inspector**

Responsibilities: Inspect materials and equipment to ensure quality standards are met, identify any flawed materials or equipment, and implement procedures to rectify quality issues

"My friends would describe me as very detail oriented."

SITUATION: "In technical school, we had a lot of group projects, and I usually did those projects with friends."

TASK: "I was typically the team member who would be in charge of quality control, fact checking, and proofreading."

ACTION: "For one project, we had to build a prototype motor to run a small windmill. I conducted much of the research and I checked all the wiring for the motor. I also formatted our schematics and proofread our final report. Because my team members knew how detail oriented I was, they were able to take more risks with the prototype design. They knew that I would go back through their work and find any mistakes they had made."

RESULTS: "As a result, our team finished the prototype early, even though we incorporated several innovative elements. We received the top score in the class, including top marks for design quality and schematic accuracy."

Write your answer to this question here:

SITUATION: _____

_____

_____

TASK: _____

_____

_____

ACTION: _____

_____

_____

_____

_____

_____

_____

RESULT: _____

_____

_____

_____

27. Persuade Me to . . .

Question: "Persuade me to open a new bank account."

Job Title: **Bank Teller**

Responsibilities: Greet customers, answer questions about their accounts, process deposits and withdrawals, and order bank cards and checks for customers

Candidate: "First, can you tell me a little about your family?"

Interviewer: "Yes, I have a husband that I've been married to for thirty years. We have two children and five grandchildren."

Candidate: "Great. Do you see your grandchildren very often?"

Interviewer: "Not as often as I'd like. My grandchildren are my pride and joy, but they live in a different state."

Candidate: "Do any of them have birthdays soon."

Interviewer: "Yes, two of them have birthdays next month."

Candidate: "Well, we have a special type of savings account that works really well for grandparents. You can set up the account in the name of your grandchildren, and you can make deposits whenever you like. It could be for birthdays, school graduations, or just to say you love them. You can open the account for as little as $20. Would you like to open accounts for your two grandchildren who have birthdays next month?"

Write your answer to this question here:

28. Estimate the Number of …

Question: "Estimate the number of seats in this city."
Question variations:
- "How many golf balls could fit in this room?"
- "How many trees are in a square mile of forest?"
- "How many blades of grass are on a football field?"

Job Title: **Freight Clerk**

Responsibilities: Maintain records of items shipped and received, organize goods in shipping and warehouse facilities, and check inventory records for accuracy

"Okay, I know there are about 200,000 people in this city. If I assume there are an average of two people per household, that means about 100,000 households. Most houses probably have three for four seats in a living room and another three or four in a dining room. Let's add three or four more seats for other rooms including chairs in bedrooms and toilets in bathrooms. Also, the average household might have two cars, so we'll add another eight seats there. Plus, most of us have chairs at work or school, so we'll add two more seats there.

"If my math is right, that's about twenty seats per household. Multiply that by 100,000 households, and you get 2,000,000 seats.

"I'd also add in seats for public venues like stadiums, theaters, and restaurant. I'd estimate four or five public venue seats per person, so that gets us to around 1,000,000 more seats. Therefore, my overall estimate is 3,000,000 seats."

Write your answer to this question here:

29. What's Your Favorite...

Question: "What's your favorite type of medication?"
Question variations: "What's your favorite advertising campaign, software program, legal argument, or power tool?"

Job Title:	**Pharmacist**
Responsibilities:	Fill prescriptions, verify physician instructions, and instruct patients on use of prescribed medicine

"I'll start with my criteria for choosing my favorite type of medication. First, it would be effective for addressing a major medical issue. Second, it would have minimal side effects. And third, it would have to be a good value compared to the benefits it provides.

"Based on those criteria, I'd have to say that my favorite type of medication is an ACE inhibitor, which is effective at treating heart disease.

"Since heart disease is the leading cause of death, it is clearly a major medical issue. Studies have shown that an ACE inhibitor is very effective at treating heart disease and extending the life expectancy of patients. Therefore, it meets my first criteria.

"It also has minimal side effects which include dizziness and drowsiness. These side effects are minor compared to the life-saving benefits it provides. Finally, at a typical cost under $500 per year, the price is minimal compared to the benefits it provides.

"Since it delivers against all three of my criteria, I'd say that an ACE inhibitor is my favorite type of medication."

Write your answer to this question here:

_____

_____

_____

_____

_____

_____

_____

_____

_____

_____

_____

_____

_____

_____

_____

_____

_____

_____

_____

30. A Disaster

Question: "While you're checking inventory in a warehouse, you notice that half of your storage boxes have been infested with termites. What would you do?"

Job Title: **Shipping and Receiving Clerk**
Responsibilities: Maintain records of all items shipped and received, compile inventory reports, check inventory records for accuracy, and organize storage areas

"First, I'd make sure all the workers in the warehouse are safe. I'd call the Center for Disease Control or a credible exterminator to ensure that a termite infestation doesn't pose a health risk. I'd also contact my manager to get authorization to get an exterminator to the site to get rid of the termites as soon as possible.

"Then, I'd work on protecting as much inventory as possible. If the inventory is something that termites could eat, like wood or paper products, I'd start inspecting boxes and move the ones that weren't infested away from the infested ones. I'd organize my co-workers to help with the inspection and moving process.

"Finally, I'd contact my counterparts in purchasing to let them know we might need to replenish our inventories. I'd also tell my sales counterparts that they may need to tell their customers that orders could be delayed while we replenish."

Write your answer to this question here:

31. Open a New Business

Question: "If I hired you to open a new business, how would you approach that?"

Job Title:	**Dentist**
Responsibilities:	Diagnose and treat issues with patients' teeth and gums, and collaborate with partners to build a successful dental practice

COMPANY: "First, I'd want to determine available resources. If I had an established dental practice, I would consider how to use the office space, equipment, and staff for the new business. Let's say I have some extra space and a biller who is great at training people to do billing. I'd consider using those resources to open a billing service."

CUSTOMER: "Next, I'd want to know as much as possible about potential customers. I have friends who are also dentists, so I'd interview them to see if they would be interested in outsourcing their billing to my new business."

COMPETITION: "I'd also want to know as much as possible about the competition. I'd research other billing services to learn about their pricing and offerings."

CONCLUSION: "Finally, I'd assess whether I could maintain a competitive advantage and charge enough to have a viable business. While my passion is for being a great dentist, I'd want someone who could manage the billing service and provide the incremental revenue stream."

Write your answer to this question here:

COMPANY: _____

_____

_____

_____

_____

_____

CUSTOMER: _____

_____

_____

_____

_____

COMPETITION: _____

_____

_____

_____

_____

CONCLUSION: _____

_____

_____

_____

_____

32. Declining Sales

Question: "Your company's sales are declining. What questions would you ask to learn why?"

Job Title:	**Butcher**
Responsibilities:	Check quality of meat, cut and grind meat, greet customers, weigh and wrap meat products, and ensure food safety standards are followed

COMPANY: "First, I'd want to know what's going on with my company. Have we changed our pricing or advertising lately? Is anything happening with our store locations? For example, is there construction near our stores that people may be trying to avoid?"

CUSTOMER: "Next, I'd want to know what's happening with our customers. Have I lost any regular customers? If so, why? Are customers changing their buying habits? For example, are they moving from red meats to white meats? If so, I might need to change my product selection."

COMPETITION: "I'd also want to know what my competitors are doing differently. Are any nearby butcher shops lowering prices? Have any competitive stores opened nearby? Are competitors offering products I don't have?"

CONCLUSION: "Based on the answers to these questions, I'd work on fixing the problem. It could involve changing advertising, pricing, or product mix. I'd consider changing whatever could get our sales back on track."

Write your answer to this question here:

COMPANY: _____
_____
_____
_____
_____
_____

CUSTOMER: _____
_____
_____
_____
_____

COMPETITION: _____
_____
_____
_____
_____

CONCLUSION: _____
_____
_____
_____
_____

33. Double Your Money

Question: "If I gave you $100, how could you double it in the next four hours?"

Job Title:	**Carpenter**
Responsibilities:	Follow blueprints and building plans, build wooden structures and fixtures, and inspect and fix damaged structures and fixtures

COMPANY: "First, I'd want to know the available resources. Let's assume I could work with your company's woodshop and equipment. If that would be okay, I'd start thinking about raw materials that I could buy for $100."

CUSTOMER: "Next, I'd want to know what my potential customers might want. Several used furniture stores are nearby, so they might want some high-quality furniture. I'd call them to see if they'd be interested in buying a dining table or maybe a nightstand. Then, I'd start working on whatever they would be willing to buy."

COMPETITION: "I'd also want to identify competitors. If there are a lot of people selling dining tables, I might decide to make a coffee table or something else that has less competition."

CONCLUSION: "Once I identified the potential customers and what they are willing to buy, I'd get to work. I could make a simple, high-quality table, deliver it to the used furniture store, collect the $200, and be back here in a few hours. How does that sound?"

Write your answer to this question here:

COMPANY: _____

_____

_____

_____

_____

_____

CUSTOMER: _____

_____

_____

_____

_____

COMPETITION: _____

_____

_____

_____

_____

CONCLUSION: _____

_____

_____

_____

_____

34. What Kind of Animal?

Question: "If you were an animal, what kind of animal would you be?"

Question variations: "What kind of plant, car, furniture, food, beverage, or movie would you be?"

Job Title:	**Home Health Aide**
Responsibilities:	Help clients with dressing and other personal tasks, check vital signs, administer medications, and assist clients with household chores

"I would be an elephant. Elephants are among the few animals that care for the older or injured members of their groups. When one elephant is moving slowly due to injury or old age, the other elephants will slow down to move at the same pace. A healthy elephant will also provide soothing sounds and gestures to an elephant that is sick or in distress.

"I also love the way elephants respect their elders. An elephant herd is typically led by the oldest female, and the other elephants will look to the elder for direction. I have tremendous respect for elders, and I have a passion for caring for people in need. Therefore, I have a lot in common with elephants."

Write your answer to this question here:

_____

_____

_____

_____

_____

_____

_____

_____

_____

_____

_____

_____

_____

_____

_____

_____

_____

_____

35. Historical Person

Question: "If you could have dinner with anyone from history, who would you choose?"

Job Title:	**Healthcare Administrator**
Responsibilities:	Identify ways to improve healthcare services, develop organizational goals and processes, and recruit and train staff

"I would choose Mother Teresa. She was a tremendous leader in the healthcare field, and I'd want to learn from her experiences.

"I've always been amazed by how much she accomplished with so little resources. She founded the Missionaries of Charity organization that now serves needy people in over a hundred countries.

"I'd ask her how she turned a small group of nuns in Calcutta into an organization that has served millions of people. I'd ask her how she recruited and trained her staff, as well as how she continuously improved and expanded her organization.

"I have a passion for providing high-quality healthcare services, and I'd love to learn from someone like Mother Teresa who created one of the most impressive service organizations in the world. I would hope that dinner with her would give me unique insight to be better in my career."

Write your answer to this question here:

_____

_____

_____

_____

_____

_____

_____

_____

_____

_____

_____

_____

_____

_____

_____

_____

_____

36. Your Most Embarrassing Moment

Question: "What was your most embarrassing moment?"

Job Title:	**Receptionist**
Responsibilities:	Answer phone calls, greet customers and guests, escort visitors to specific destinations, and schedule appointments

SITUATION: "My most embarrassing moment was when I was working as a receptionist at a large corporate office building."

TASK: "One of my tasks was to escort guests from the reception area to meetings in the building."

ACTION: "One day, a visitor from overseas arrived, and he asked me to show him to Mr. Baxter, our chief executive officer. I escorted the visitor to the executive offices, where I introduced him to Mr. Baxter. They stared at me with confused looks on their faces. After some discussion, we figured out the visitor wanted to be shown to the bathroom, not Mr. Baxter. I misunderstood his request."

RESULT: "Fortunately, Mr. Baxter was a good sport about my confusing his name with the word *bathroom*. We all had a good laugh, and I've learned to be more careful. Now, I always make sure I understand exactly what guests want, and I double-check their requests before acting."

Write your answer to this question here:

SITUATION: _____

_____

_____

TASK: _____

_____

_____

ACTION: _____

_____

_____

_____

_____

_____

_____

RESULT: _____

_____

_____

_____

37. You as a Child

Question: "What were you like as a child?"

Job Title:	**Mechanic**
Responsibilities:	Diagnose issues and repair vehicles, perform maintenance procedures, and explain vehicle issues and repair options to clients

PASSION: "I've always loved repairing things."

EXPERIENCE: "When I was a child, I spent hours playing with mechanical sets and fixing toys. While my friends were playing sports and watching TV, I would be taking my toys apart and figuring out how to put them back together.

"By the time I was in middle school, I was repairing bikes for my friends whenever they needed it. I was also fixing anything from broken action figures to damaged skateboards.

"In high school, I even earned first place in our district's science fair by repairing an old windmill so it could generate electricity on windy days."

NEXT: "Now, I'm looking for a job where I can turn my passion for repairing things into a career. Hopefully, I can do that by working for you."

Write your answer to this question here:

PASSION: _____

_____

_____

EXPERIENCE: _____

_____

_____

_____

_____

_____

_____

_____

NEXT: _____

_____

_____

_____

_____

_____

38. Your Favorite Book or Movie

Question: "What is your favorite movie?"

Job Title:	**Human Resources Specialist**
Responsibilities:	Recruit candidates for employment, consult on hiring decisions, provide new employee orientation, and assist employees with personnel issues and employment benefit needs

PASSION: "I love books and movies that show the human struggle, especially in the workplace. My favorite movie is *Up in the Air* because it shows how challenging things can get for employees who are impacted by layoffs."

EXPERIENCE: "The main character, who is played by George Clooney, makes his living by flying around the country and handling layoffs for companies. It's his job to tell employees that they no longer have jobs. He's able to do this very effectively because he persuades people that the layoffs are good for them because of the new opportunities that will be available for them. I'll try not to ruin the plot if you haven't seen the movie, but I will tell you that I learned a lot from the movie about how to make sure you follow up on clues that people give you about their emotions."

NEXT: "I'm looking for a role where I can help people with their struggles in the workplace. I believe we all deserve to feel valued for what we contribute, and I want to be in a career in which I can help people get the most out of their work experience and make the biggest possible contributions to their employer."

Write your answer to this question here:

PASSION: _____

_____

_____

EXPERIENCE: _____

_____

_____

_____

_____

_____

_____

_____

_____

NEXT: _____

_____

_____

_____

_____

39. Who Inspires You?

Question: "Who inspires you?"

Job Title:	**Housekeeper**
Responsibilities:	Clean rooms, make beds, sweep and vacuum, dust surfaces, clean windows

"I really admire my grandfather. He was the hardest working person I've ever known. He was the janitor for a large school, and he took great pride in his work.

"When I was young, he used to take me to work with him. I would do my homework while he cleaned the school. When I finished my homework, he would show me how to clean floors properly and get tough stains out of carpets. He had so much knowledge about cleaning and making minor repairs that he always impressed me.

"He taught me the value of leaving a workplace in spotless condition. Every evening when we finished his cleaning, he would go back through each room to make sure he hadn't missed anything. He would wipe down surfaces one last time and straighten chairs that were out of place.

"My mother says that's where I get my attention to detail. And to this day, I still walk through every room when I'm done cleaning to make sure everything is spotless and in order. That's how I honor the man who inspires me, my grandfather."

Write your answer to this question here:

40. Your Tagline

Question: "If you were a brand, what would your tagline be?"

Job Title: **Professor**

Responsibilities: Teach college students in specialized subject matter, help students increase their knowledge, and develop lesson plans and assignments

"For my tagline, I'd go with *Teaching high-level math with down-to-earth applications*. While I enjoy teaching theoretical concepts, I love showing students how to apply those concepts to the real world. That's why I've always had a project element to my classes.

"Last year, I taught advanced mathematics to engineering students. That subject is highly theoretical. To help them learn to apply the topic, each student needed to define a project where they could apply the principles I taught in class.

"Students came up with projects that involved everything from modeling population growth for city planners to calculating life expectancies for insurance companies. Other projects included determining the thrust needed for jet engines and identifying the load bearing capabilities of various construction materials.

"When my students interviewed for jobs, they often used their class projects as examples of their skills, which helped them get the jobs they wanted. Because I like to apply learning to real world situations, I like the tagline *Teaching high-level math with down-to-earth applications*."

Write your answer to this question here:

_____

_____

_____

_____

_____

_____

_____

_____

_____

_____

_____

_____

_____

_____

_____

_____

_____

41. Anything Else

Question: "Is there anything else I should know about you?"

Job Title:	**Surveyor**
Responsibilities:	Conduct measurements to identify precise locations for construction activity, prepare maps and plots, and present findings to supervisors

"One thing we haven't discussed is what I might consider my biggest accomplishment."

SITUATION: "A few years ago, I was a surveyor for a road construction company."

TASK: "My assignment was to plot the best route for a road through terrain that had bogs and sinkholes."

ACTIONS: "I had read about a new technology that maps the density of material below the earth's surface. Since I was worried about building the road on unstable land, I persuaded my supervisor to try the new technology. I contacted the company that provided the technology, and I persuaded them to give us one project for free. If we liked the results, we would use them on future projects."

RESULT: "As a result, we found several large underground caverns that could have been major obstacles during the construction process. By identifying those caverns before construction started, I saved the company approximately $1 million in construction costs and three months in project time."

Write your answer to this question here:

42. References

Question: "Do you have references?"

Job Title:	**Pilot**
Responsibilities:	Conduct aircraft inspections and other pre-flight procedures, operate aircraft during takeoffs and landings, operate and navigate aircraft during flights and taxiing, and maintain all required flight records

"Yes, here is my list of references. The first person was my supervisor at my last job. I worked for her for three years, so she can speak to my performance as a pilot.

"The next person on the list was my instructor in flight school. He is familiar with the skills I demonstrated during my training, including my ability to handle challenging situations that I encountered during simulation training.

"The third person on the list was my lieutenant when I was in the air force. He is familiar with my military training, and he can speak to my ability to handle complex aircraft and stressful situations.

"Next to each person's name, I've listed their preferred way to be contacted. They've agreed to be references for me, so feel free to contact them at your convenience."

Write your answer to this question here:

43. What Questions Do You Have?

Question: "What questions do you have?"

Job Title: **Medical Secretary**

Responsibilities: Answer phone calls, record patient information and messages, schedule appointments, and update information in medical databases

"I noticed that your company was recently recognized as a top place to work. What are some of the reasons it's such a great place to work?"

"Why did you choose to work for this company?"

"How has your organization been able to deliver such impressive growth?"

Write your answer to this question here:

44. When Can You Start?

Question: "When can you start?"

Job Title:	**Nursing Aide and Orderly**
Responsibilities:	Help patients with bathing and other personal tasks, change linens, monitor health status of patients, measure vital signs, serve meals, and help patients eat

"Once we negotiate a favorable offer, I'd immediately give notice to my current employer. I'm required to give two weeks of notice, so I'd need to remain for those two weeks to help them transition my responsibilities to someone else.

"Since I'll be moving from another city, I'd like a few days to move my belongings before I start work. Ideally, that would mean I could start working three weeks after accepting your offer. Would that work for you?"

Write your answer to this question here:

_____

_____

_____

_____

_____

_____

_____

_____

_____

_____

_____

_____

_____

_____

_____

_____

_____

_____

Sample Job Descriptions

This section contains sample job descriptions for a wide variety of occupations. You can find hundreds of additional job descriptions on the Bureau of Labor Statistics website (www.bls.gov/ooh). The information on the following pages is from my research on the BLS site in just a few hours. If you don't see the type of job you want on the following pages, I recommend you go to the BLS site and research the specific occupations that appeal to you.

Now, take a few minutes to research job descriptions in your desired occupation and write the key details below. Before you go to a job interview, I recommend you read the job description for that specific role and update the key details on this form. Then, refer to this form as you prepare your answers to the interview questions in this book.

Job Title: _____

Responsibilities: _____

_____

_____

_____

_____

_____

_____

Education Level: _____

_____

Job Title:	**Accountant**
Responsibilities:	Organize and maintain financial records, recommend improvements to business processes, identify ways to increase revenue and reduce costs
Education Level:	Bachelor's degree in accounting

Job Title:	**Administrative Assistant**
Responsibilities:	Organize files, schedule appointments, prepare expense reports, and perform other administrative tasks
Education Level:	High school diploma or equivalent may be required

Job Title:	**Agency Account Manager**
Responsibilities:	Manage relationships with clients, manage agency team, and plan projects related to the development of marketing programs
Education Level:	Bachelor's degree in marketing or related field

Job Title:	**Arbitrator**
Responsibilities:	Facilitate communication between disputing parties, clarify issues and interests of involved parties, and guide discussions to mutually acceptable agreements
Education Level:	Associate's or bachelor's degree in conflict resolution, counseling, or related field

Job Title:	**Architect**
Responsibilities:	Create building designs using computer-aided design (CAD) applications, prepare project reports, and research building codes
Education Level:	Bachelor's degree in architecture

Job Title:	**Assembler and Fabricator**
Responsibilities:	Read assembly instructions and blueprints, use hand tools and power tools to assemble parts, and conduct quality control checks
Education Level:	High school diploma or equivalent may be required

Job Title:	**Attorney**
Responsibilities:	Represent clients on legal matters, research laws and regulations, communicate with clients and judges, prepare and file legal documents, and present evidence in writing and verbally
Education Level:	Juris Doctor (J.D.) degree from accredited law school

Job Title:	**Baker**
Responsibilities:	Check quality of baking ingredients, bake variety of breads and other baked goods, decorate food items, maintain safety standards, and prepare and clean baking equipment
Education Level:	Degree from technical or culinary school may be preferred

Job Title:	**Bank Teller**
Responsibilities:	Greet customers, answer questions about their accounts, process deposits and withdrawals, and order bank cards and checks for customers
Education Level:	High school diploma or equivalent

Job Title:	**Bookkeeper**
Responsibilities:	Work with accounting software, document financial transactions, organize and analyze data, and develop financial recommendations
Education Level:	Bachelor's degree in accounting

Job Title:	**Butcher**
Responsibilities:	Check quality of meat, cut and grind meat, greet customers, weigh and wrap meat products, clean and maintain equipment, and ensure food safety standards are followed
Education Level:	No formal education typically required

Job Title:	**Cafeteria Worker**
Responsibilities:	Prepare and cook food, greet and serve customers, and clean work areas and cooking equipment
Education Level:	No formal education typically required

Job Title:	**Carpenter**
Responsibilities:	Follow blueprints and building plans, build wooden structures and fixtures, and inspect and fix damaged structures and fixtures
Education Level:	Vocational classes in carpentry preferred

Job Title:	**Childcare Worker**
Responsibilities:	Supervise and maintain safety of children, organize activities to entertain and educate children, serve food and change diapers as needed, and keep records of progress and issues with children
Education Level:	High school diploma preferred, background check and state licensing often required

Job Title:	**Civil Engineer**
Responsibilities:	Plan construction projects for commercial buildings, inspect construction sites, and monitor project progress
Education Level:	Bachelor's degree in civil engineering

Job Title:	**Computer Programmer**
Responsibilities:	Write and test code for computer applications and integrate work with coding from other programmers
Education Level:	Bachelor's degree in computer science or software engineering

Job Title:	**Computer Software Developer**
Responsibilities:	Design computer applications, test software, identify program flaws, and implement patches
Education Level:	Bachelor's degree in computer science or software engineering

Job Title:	**Computer Systems Administrator**
Responsibilities:	Design and install computer systems, identify ways to improve system effectiveness and efficiency, and troubleshoot computer issues
Education Level:	Bachelor's degree in computer science or related field

Job Title:	**Computer Technician**
Responsibilities:	Install and repair computer hardware, install and update software, troubleshoot computer issues, and provide technical support to company personnel
Education Level:	Degree from associate's program or technical school

Job Title:	**Construction Worker**
Responsibilities:	Follow construction plans and supervisor's instructions to build structures, load and unload building materials, operate tools needed during construction process, and clean and organize construction sites as needed
Education Level:	No formal education typically required

214

Job Title:	**Consultant**
Responsibilities:	Gather information about organizations, analyze business situations, and recommend new strategies to improve performance
Education Level:	Bachelor's degree in business or related field

Job Title:	**Cook**
Responsibilities:	Check freshness of food ingredients, prepare food based on customer orders, and clean food preparation areas
Education Level:	Associate's degree or vocational school degree in culinary arts may be preferred

Job Title:	**Creative Director**
Responsibilities:	Train and supervise staff on creative design techniques, determine design elements needed to bring ideas to life, develop project timelines and budgets, and present designs to clients for approval
Education Level:	Bachelor's degree in graphic design

Job Title:	**Data Analyst**
Responsibilities:	Analyze data, evaluate financial information, study industry trends, and prepare proposals for improving business results
Education Level:	Bachelor's degree in finance, statistics, mathematics, or related field

Job Title:	**Delivery Person**
Responsibilities:	Load and unload cargo, drive variety of delivery vehicles, document deliveries, and accept payments for shipments
Education Level:	High school diploma or equivalent may be preferred, valid driver's license required

Job Title:	**Dentist**
Responsibilities:	Diagnose and treat issues with patients' teeth and gums and collaborate with partners to build a successful dental practice
Education Level:	Doctorate degree from accredited dental program, valid state dental license

Job Title:	**Detective**
Responsibilities:	Analyze crime scenes, collect evidence, interview witnesses and suspects, solve crimes, and testify in court
Education Level:	Degree from police academy or similar training program

Job Title:	**Electrical Engineer**
Responsibilities:	Design electrical systems and electronic products, evaluate electrical components, and recommend design improvements
Education Level:	Bachelor's degree in electrical engineering

Job Title:	**Events Planner**
Responsibilities:	Develop agendas, room designs, meeting schedules, attendee lists, and invitations for major corporate events; negotiate contracts, and manage event timelines and budgets
Education Level:	Bachelor's degree may be preferred

Job Title:	**Finance Manager**
Responsibilities:	Analyze financial information, determine effectiveness of investments, and prepare recommendations for allocating budgets and improving investment returns
Education Level:	Master's degree in finance

Job Title:	**Freight Clerk**
Responsibilities:	Maintain records of items shipped and received, organize goods in shipping and warehouse facilities, and check inventory records for accuracy
Education Level:	High school diploma or equivalent

Job Title:	**General Manager**
Responsibilities:	Define the priorities of the organization, oversee the budget and staffing activities, make staffing decisions for leadership team, evaluate and approve key projects and investments
Education Level:	Bachelor's or master's degree in business

Job Title:	**Graphic Designer**
Responsibilities:	Work with design software, create compelling visual concepts, develop impactful layouts, and prepare graphic files for production
Education Level:	Associate's or bachelor's degree in graphic design may be required

Job Title:	**Healthcare Administrator**
Responsibilities:	Identify ways to improve healthcare services, develop organizational goals and processes, and recruit and train staff
Education Level:	Master's degree in health administration or related field

Job Title:	**Home Health Aide**
Responsibilities:	Help clients with dressing and other personal tasks, check vital signs, administer medications, and assist clients with household chores
Education Level:	High school diploma or equivalent preferred, background check and state licensing required

Job Title:	**Housekeeper**
Responsibilities:	Clean rooms, make beds, sweep and vacuum, dust surfaces, and clean windows
Education Level:	No formal education typically required

Job Title:	**Human Resources Specialist**
Responsibilities:	Recruit candidates for employment, conduct job interviews, contact references, consult on hiring decisions, provide new employee orientation, and assist employees with personnel issues
Education Level:	Bachelor's degree in human resources or related field

Job Title:	**Innovation Director**
Responsibilities:	Identify new product lines or new benefits for existing products, determine market potential for new items, and build project plans
Education Level:	Bachelor's degree in related field

Job Title:	**Insights Manager**
Responsibilities:	Analyze trends and competitive landscapes, identify business opportunities, and recommend improvements to marketing programs
Education Level:	Bachelor's degree in consumer insights or related field

Job Title:	**Janitor and Building Cleaner**
Responsibilities:	Gather and empty trash, sweep and mop floors, clean restrooms, order cleaning supplies, notify maintenance personnel when repairs are needed, and lock building doors
Education Level:	No formal education typically required

Job Title:	**Logistics Manager**
Responsibilities:	Determine most efficient methods for transporting goods, identify ways to reduce costs and increase speed of delivery, and address logistical issues as they arise
Education Level:	Associate's degree in systems engineering, supply chain management, or related field

Job Title:	**Marketing Assistant**
Responsibilities:	Identify marketing campaign ideas, write agency briefs, and manage cross-functional project teams
Education Level:	Bachelor's degree in marketing or related field

Job Title:	**Marketing Manager**
Responsibilities:	Manage team of marketing staff, develop advertising strategies and media plans, evaluate marketing campaign elements, and determine team staffing needs and budget allocations
Education Level:	Master's degree with emphasis in marketing

Job Title:	**Mechanic**
Responsibilities:	Diagnose issues and repair vehicles, perform maintenance procedures, explain vehicle issues and repair options to clients
Education Level:	Vocational training in vehicle mechanics preferred

Job Title:	**Mechanical Engineer**
Responsibilities:	Design mechanical systems and devices, develop and test prototypes, and oversee manufacturing process
Education Level:	Bachelor's degree in engineering

Job Title:	**Medical Assistant**
Responsibilities:	Interview patients, record medical histories, measure vital signs, assist with patient exams, give patients medications and injections, and enter information in medical records
Education Level:	Associate's degree in medical assisting

Job Title:	**Medical Secretary**
Responsibilities:	Answer phones, record patient information and messages, schedule appointments, and update information in medical databases
Education Level:	High school diploma or equivalent required, some training or experience in medical field preferred

Job Title:	**Nurse**
Responsibilities:	Evaluate patients, record medical histories and symptoms, administer medicines and treatments, and consult with doctors and other health professionals
Education Level:	Degree from an approved nursing program

Job Title:	**Nursing Aide and Orderly**
Responsibilities:	Help patients with bathing and other personal tasks, change linens, monitor health status of patients, and help patients eat
Education Level:	State approved nursing assistant training, nursing assistant license required in some states

Job Title:	**Office Clerk**
Responsibilities:	Answer phone calls, take messages, schedule appointments, greet visitors, and prepare letters and other office documents
Education Level:	High school diploma or equivalent

Job Title:	**Office Manager**
Responsibilities:	Organize office operations and procedures, supervise all clerical procedures, and manage the recruiting and training for all office staff
Education Level:	Bachelor's degree in business or related field

Job Title:	**Painter**
Responsibilities:	Prepare rooms by covering surfaces, fill holes in walls, prepare surfaces by sanding and scraping loose paint, apply primers and paint, and clean rooms after painting procedures are complete
Education Level:	No formal education typically required

Job Title:	**Paralegal**
Responsibilities:	Research laws and regulations, help attorneys prepare for trials, get affidavits to be used as evidence, and file briefs with the court
Education Level:	Associate's or bachelor's degree in paralegal studies

Job Title:	**Personal Care Aide**
Responsibilities:	Assist clients with daily tasks, engage clients with physical and mental activity, perform basic housekeeping tasks, prepare and serve meals, and assist clients with shopping and bill paying
Education Level:	High school diploma or equivalent, first aid certification preferred

Job Title:	**Pharmaceutical Sales Representative**
Responsibilities:	Build relationships with healthcare providers, sell portfolio of pharmaceutical products, resolve customer inquiries and complaints, and document all customer interactions
Education Level:	Bachelor's degree

Job Title:	**Pharmacist**
Responsibilities:	Fill prescriptions, verify physician instructions, and inform patients on use of medications
Education Level:	Doctor of Pharmacy degree

Job Title:	**Physician**
Responsibilities:	Diagnose and treat medical issues, order and interpret medical tests, develop treatment plans, and educate patients on treatment plans
Education Level:	Degree from accredited medical school, certification from state medical board

Job Title:	**Physician Assistant**
Responsibilities:	Interview patients, perform physical examinations, administer diagnostic tests, and consult with physician on diagnosing and treating medical conditions
Education Level:	Master's degree in physician assistant studies

Job Title:	**Pilot**
Responsibilities:	Conduct aircraft inspections and other pre-flight procedures, operate aircraft during takeoffs and landings, navigate aircraft during flights and taxiing, and maintain all required flight records
Education Level:	Pilot's license required; bachelor's degree may be required

Job Title:	**Police Officer**
Responsibilities:	Enforce laws, respond to emergency calls, patrol areas, conduct traffic stops, issue citations, interview victims, witnesses and suspects, gather evidence, and testify in court
Education Level:	Degree from police academy or similar program

Job Title:	**Production Manager**
Responsibilities:	Supervise production workers, ensure proper staffing of plant operations, ensure production goals are met, and ensure safety of all workers
Education Level:	Bachelor's degree in industrial engineering or similar field

Job Title:	**Professor**
Responsibilities:	Teach college students in specialized subject matter, work with students to improve their knowledge, and develop lesson plans
Education Level:	Master's or doctorate degree in related field

Job Title:	**Psychiatrist**
Responsibilities:	Diagnose and treat patients who have cognitive or emotional challenges, and collaborate with other medical experts to provide treatment plans
Education Level:	Doctorate degree in psychology

Job Title:	**Public Relations Manager**
Responsibilities:	Develop public relations strategy and tactics, write and distribute press releases, and lead social media efforts
Education Level:	Bachelor's degree in communications or related field

Job Title:	**Purchasing Agent**
Responsibilities:	Determine supply and equipment needs, identify and maintain relationships with suppliers, and negotiate prices and delivery contracts
Education Level:	Bachelor's degree in supply management or related field

Job Title:	**Quality Control Inspector**
Responsibilities:	Inspect materials and equipment to ensure quality standard are met, identify flawed materials or equipment, and implement procedures to rectify quality issues
Education Level:	High school diploma or equivalent

Job Title:	**Radio Talk Show Host**
Responsibilities:	Announce radio station programming, comment on current events, interview guests, and entertain audience
Education Level:	Bachelor's degree in journalism, broadcasting, or related field

Job Title:	**Receptionist**
Responsibilities:	Answer telephone calls, greet guests, escort visitors to specific destinations, schedule appointments, and maintain office records
Education Level:	High school diploma or equivalent often required

Job Title:	**Reporter**
Responsibilities:	Research topics, interview people, write articles, edit, and submit articles prior to publication deadlines
Education Level:	Bachelor's degree in journalism, communication, or related field

Job Title:	**Sales Manager**
Responsibilities:	Manage team of sales representatives, set sales goals and motivate team members to deliver results, and make personnel decisions for team including hiring, firing, and promotion decisions
Education Level:	Bachelor's degree

Job Title:	**Sales Representative**
Responsibilities:	Work with potential and existing customers, meet sales objectives, and build lasting relationships
Education Level:	Bachelor's degree

Job Title:	**Sales Vice President**
Responsibilities:	Lead sales strategy for department of forty employees, determine recruiting and training needs for department, and make changes to department's organizational structure as needed
Education Level:	Master's degree may be required

Job Title:	**Salesperson**
Responsibilities:	Greet customers, process sales transactions, suggest upsell items, and answer customer questions
Education Level:	High school diploma or equivalent

Job Title:	**Security Guard**
Responsibilities:	Provide security and enforce laws on employer's property, monitor alarms and surveillance cameras, and conduct security checks
Education Level:	High school diploma or equivalent may be required; state certification with background check

Job Title:	**Shift Manager**
Responsibilities:	Lead personnel when manager or assistant manager is not present, assign tasks and delegate duties to all employees on shift, and resolve any customer issues
Education Level:	High school diploma or equivalent

Job Title:	**Shipping and Receiving Clerk**
Responsibilities:	Maintain records of all items shipped and received, compile inventory reports, check inventory records for accuracy, and organize storage areas
Education Level:	High school diploma or equivalent

Job Title:	**Store Clerk**
Responsibilities:	Greet customers and answer their questions, recommend merchandise to meet customer needs, process payment transactions, and restock items as needed
Education Level:	No formal education typically needed

Job Title:	**Store Manager**
Responsibilities:	Ensure proper operations of store, supervise staff, conduct hiring and training procedures, resolve customer complaints, and ensure store delivers on sales goals and budget numbers
Education Level:	Bachelor's degree in business management or related field

Job Title:	**Strategy Director**
Responsibilities:	Lead strategic projects, manage teams of external consultants, and develop recommendations for new business models, present to executives
Education Level:	Master's degree with emphasis in business strategy or finance

Job Title:	**Surveyor**
Responsibilities:	Conduct measurement procedures to determine property boundaries, research land titles and survey records, and prepare maps and plots
Education Level:	Bachelor's degree in engineering or related field

Job Title:	**Tax Accountant**
Responsibilities:	Prepare tax returns, meet with clients to discuss tax matters, and conduct training programs for tax regulations and software programs
Education Level:	Bachelor's degree in accounting

Job Title:	**Teacher**
Responsibilities:	Create lesson plans, teach and evaluate students, develop strategies to address individual student abilities and issues, grade assignments, and maintain order in the classroom
Education Level:	Bachelor's degree in education

Job Title:	**Teaching Assistant**
Responsibilities:	Tutor students, supervise students when teacher is unavailable, and help teacher prepare lessons and grade papers
Education Level:	Associate's or bachelor's degree for teacher assistants preferred

Job Title:	**Truck Driver**
Responsibilities:	Inspect truck and trailer before and after trips, drive long distances, comply with all traffic laws, maintain vehicle in good working order, and maintain log of driving time and incidents
Education Level:	High school diploma or equivalent preferred, commercial driver's license required

Job Title:	**Waiter or Waitress**
Responsibilities:	Greet customers, present menus, answer questions about menu items, take food and beverage orders, deliver food from kitchen area, prepare checks, and take payments from customers
Education Level:	No formal education typically needed

Job Title:	**Welder**
Responsibilities:	Read blueprints and design specifications, weld metal parts together, and maintain equipment
Education Level:	High school diploma or equivalent preferred, trade school training preferred

Acknowledgements

I'd like to thank my lovely wife who gave me the idea for this book and the encouragement I needed throughout the writing process. She's also supported me over the years while I've traveled to college campuses to interview job candidates and lead interview training workshops.

I'd also like to thank Eric Bishop, my co-author on my first book. He introduced me to Fiverr.com, Freelancer.com, and other tools that have been invaluable in the book publishing process.

I had two fabulous editors for this book, Trisha Alcisto (www.trishaalcisto.me) and qdmerit (qdmerit@fiverr.com). The book cover was designed by a talented graphic artist, Mercedes Piñera (www.behance.net/espacio_M).

The audio version of this book was narrated by Chris Abernathy (www.AbernathyVoice.com). He did an amazing job of bringing this book to life in audio format.

Finally, thank you for taking the time to read this book. I would appreciate it if you entered a rating and a review on the site where you purchased this book.

About the Author

Richard Blazevich has led the campus recruiting efforts for the marketing department of a multinational consumer products company. Over the years, he has interviewed hundreds of candidates for a wide variety of roles. He has also developed and led interview training workshops for students at some of the top business schools in the United States.

Richard is a senior director of marketing with over 15 years of experience. He received an MBA with an emphasis in Marketing and Business Strategy from the University of Michigan and a Bachelor's degree in Business from Montana State University.

If you've enjoyed this book, here are other books by this author that you might want to read.

Start-to-Finish Job Search Guide

Book 1 in the Start-to-Finish Series

Learn everything you'll need to know to get your dream job. This book explains how to prepare your job search strategy, customize your resume, and nail your interviews. It contains a step-by-step plan to help you get the job you want.

Start-to-Finish Resume Guide

Book 2 in the Start-to-Finish Series

Discover how to write a winning resume. Get step-by-step instructions for building the perfect resume for the job you want. You'll learn tricks like key word stuffing and rapid customization to give you a competitive advantage in even the most challenging job market.

Start-to-Finish Job Search Workbook

Book 3 in the Start-to-Finish Series

Discover how to write a winning resume. Get step-by-step instructions for building the perfect resume for the job you want. You'll learn tricks like key word stuffing and rapid customization to give you a competitive advantage in even the most challenging job market.

Start-to-Finish Job Search Guide

College Student Edition

This book is designed to help college students get their first big job. It provides easy-to-follow instructions for researching companies, perfecting resumes, nailing job interviews, and every other step in the job search process.

That's a Bullseye

Learn how to create an effective marketing campaign and connect with your most important customers. This book provides a practical approach for building a marketing strategy.

Made in the USA
Las Vegas, NV
28 April 2021